OLD-TIME WOODCUTS
From the Nineteenth-Century Stage

From THE LOTTERY OF LIFE (see No. 107).

OLD-TIME WOODCUTS

From the Nineteenth-Century Stage

268 Copyright-free Illustrations
for Artists and Designers

Selected and Edited by
STANLEY APPELBAUM

Dover Publications, Inc.
New York

Published in Canada by General Publishing Company, Ltd., 30 Lesmill Road, Don Mills, Toronto, Ontario.
Published in the United Kingdom by Constable and Company, Ltd., 10 Orange Street, London WC2H 7EG.

Old-Time Woodcuts from the Nineteenth-Century Stage: 268 Copyright-free Illustrations for Artists and Designers, formerly published by Dover under the titles *Scenes from the Nineteenth-Century Stage in Advertising Woodcuts* (1977) and *Advertising Woodcuts from the Nineteenth-Century Stage* (1980), first published by Dover Publications, Inc., in 1977, is a new selection of illustrations from the work *Specimens of Theatrical Cuts* (full title in Introduction), originally published by the Ledger Job Printing Office, Philadelphia, ca. 1875. All the text in the present volume is new and specially prepared for the Dover edition.

DOVER *Pictorial Archive* SERIES

International Standard Book Number: 0-486-23434-7
Library of Congress Catalog Card Number: 76-19998

Manufactured in the United States of America
Dover Publications, Inc.
31 East 2nd Street
Mineola, N.Y. 11501

PREFACE AND ACKNOWLEDGMENTS

The woodcuts in this volume, all from one old pictorial catalogue of theatrical cuts, are fascinating and diverting even when looked at simply as pictures or seen within the general context of early advertising art—and the reader is warmly urged to enjoy and perhaps make further use of them as such. But great credit is due to the publisher, Hayward Cirker, for envisioning the book as a contribution to theater history, and I am grateful for his invitation to organize the material in this light.

Much—one might say almost all—of the serious investigation of nineteenth-century theater remains to be done, and even the admirable multivolume works of Allardyce Nicoll (*A History of English Drama 1660–1900*) and George C. D. Odell (*Annals of the New York Stage*) are incomplete in the mere registration of the titles of plays and shows produced in London and New York. Not having undertaken any archival research (though I consulted many published and unpublished play texts, promptbooks, programs and reviews, as well as books of theatrical history, biography and reminiscences), all I can claim is to have divided the pictures into useful categories, identifying playwrights in most cases, and adding a miscellany of other information, in hopes of providing a working tool of first resort to scholars (since the pictures are truly primary material), a supplementary aid for teachers, or a collection of sufficient interest to general readers in the area.

Most of the statistics I have supplied will be found quite reliable. A few of the dates, particularly for American premières of English plays, may be subject to revision. Where conflicting statements existed about French sources of plays, I have entered only those that seemed fairly certain; I have not attempted to track down every last one, though I believe one or two may be given here for the first time. My doubts on various points are expressed in the Additional Comments.

I trust that my identification of the specific action shown in the cuts will be found helpful; but it must be remembered that play texts were far from sacrosanct in the nineteenth century

ABOVE: *Agnes Robertson, wife of Dion Boucicault and star of many of his plays.* BELOW: *The important leading man Edwin Adams in the title role of "Enoch Arden."*

and that, in practice, variations in act divisions or even in plot situations were frequent. The Additional Comments point out each case in which my descriptions are not derived from an English-language play text or promptbook, but instead from a foreign original, a novel or a program or review.

Many of the plays and other matter were consulted in the Theatre Collection of the New York Public Library at Lincoln Center; I wish to thank the staff for their assistance.

All the pictorial matter reproduced within the Introduction is from my collection.

S. A.

New York, N.Y.
May 1976

INTRODUCTION

In this day of films and television, in which the scope of the theater is being increasingly reduced to that of a rare costly treat for well-to-do people in metropolises or academic oases, it is difficult to imagine the predominant part it played in the lives of Americans in the second half of the nineteenth century. Juliets and jugglers both had their audiences in the big city or in the tiniest village meetinghouse that could possibly yield enough cash to keep a stagestruck novice's body and soul together. Road transportation, canal barges, river steamboats and railroads brought the theater to every part of the country, and many performers and vehicles "caught on" nationally with startling rapidity. In the cities, theaters were large and the price of admission low, so that any newsboy could envy the hero from the topmost gallery at least once a week.

The offerings in such urban centers as New York, Boston, Philadelphia, Baltimore, Chicago, St. Louis, New Orleans and San Francisco were enormously varied, especially since long runs were not yet customary and programs changed frequently. English and Continental celebrities were often on hand to demonstrate their special talents and repertoire, and to gather in the greenbacks. On the other hand, audiences would attend certain standard plays (and not only Shakespeare's) over and over again to see how different Thespians delivered the well-known lines—just as operagoers even today will compare many different singers in the same familiar roles. Problem plays appeared only sporadically before the end of the century; thrills, laughter and spectacle were the rule, and even the critics could understand what a show was about.

It is this happy time that is recorded graphically in the present book, which contains a large selection of woodcuts from the work *Specimens of Theatrical Cuts/ Being Fac-Similes, in Miniature, of/ Poster Cuts;/ Comprising Colored and Plain Designs,/ Suitable for/ Theatrical, Variety and Circus Business/ Also, a Large Variety of/ Programme and Card Cuts, Lithographs, etc.,/ to Be Had at the/ Ledger Job Printing Office,/ Public*

ABOVE: *George L. Fox, the great American pantomime clown who starred in "Humpty Dumpty."*
BELOW: *Pauline Markham, one of Lydia Thompson's original "British Blondes"; she played Venus in "Ixion."*

Ledger Building,/ Philadelphia./ George W. Childs, Proprietor./ J. H. Alexander, Business Manager.

Though undated, the edition used here may safely be assigned to the year 1875, since the two latest plays represented in it, *The Two Orphans* and *The Three Dwarfs*, both opened in New York on December 21, 1874.* A copy in the Theatre Collection of The New York Public Library at Lincoln Center, evidently from the same edition, includes a play that opened in November 1875; this means either that a few pages were inserted later in the Library's copy or that the copy serving as the basis for the present volume was slightly defective. The Lincoln Center collection also contains another, mangled, copy of the work, with a somewhat different title, dated 1869; perhaps this was the first edition. In addition, a still later edition was reprinted in Hollywood a few years ago by Cherokee Books; this is incorrectly dated "1869 and 1872" by the reprint publisher, since it contains a number of plays that did not appear until well into the 1880s. (The Ledger Job Printing Office also published a similar, but much slenderer, volume in 1868 devoted to minstrel cuts; hence the almost total absence of minstrelsy from the present collection.)

This Philadelphia printing firm (attached to a newspaper, like so many at the time) was a major supplier of theatrical posters in the 1860s and 1870s, and its work was to be seen far and wide. Although it did produce some lithographs, the art was mainly in somewhat crude, though highly flavorful, woodcut. This was typical of American poster art (especially theatrical) of the time, which still lagged far behind France and England technically; it was not until the 1880s that lithography was the rule in American theater posters.

In the woodcut process, color is achieved by successive application of separate blocks. Even the miniaturizations of color posters in the Ledger Job Printing Office's pictorial catalogue or specimen book (hereafter called "the catalogue" for brevity) appeared in color, but, apart from a few examples on the covers, the present volume has, in the interests of clarity and definition, employed only black-and-white line reproduction.

The offerings of this firm were "stock posters," that is, posters manufactured on speculation and sold in quantity as called for, the purchasers then inserting any special typography they required. Within the original catalogue, there was no text other than a brief (and sometimes inaccurate) title of the play illustrated and an indication of the size and coloring of the poster or program cut (with price) available for that illustration. Nor was there any organization except by printer's categories: color poster cuts, black-and-white poster cuts, program cuts and the like. The section "Illustrations by Printer's Categories," to be

TOP TO BOTTOM: *The famous actress-manager Laura Keene, who first staged "Our American Cousin"; E. A. Sothern, who created the role of Lord Dundreary in that play; and Lester Wallack, New York actor-manager and playwright.*

* *Lady Clancarty*, which opened in London on March 9, 1874, was apparently not seen in the New York area (Brooklyn) until January 4, 1875, but it may very well have been produced earlier elsewhere in the United States.

found later in this volume, indicates, for each illustration included here, the size, the number of colors and the price (in 1875), and information on sheet sizes. It will be noticed that, in general, the very large posters were for musical extravaganzas rather than for straight plays. (Incidentally, some posters in this period were made up of montages of the miniature cuts themselves.)

The original catalogue was addressed, as its brief "Explanatory Note" made clear, to "Managers and Agents." In this period, "manager" would mean not only the man in charge of a theater building; it was even more likely to denote the man in charge of a traveling company. The great era of "the road" in American theater was already in full swing, thanks to the great expansion of railroads and, consequently, of theater construction. The "agent" that was meant was the advance agent, a significant individual (many advance agents became top-flight managers) who traveled a step ahead of the touring company, renting the next theater and making sure it was ready for the type of performance required, reserving hotel rooms, and—very important—billing the town with the stock posters.

The great value of the catalogue to us today is twofold. For one thing, it gives a good indication of which plays were popular and the relative magnitude of their popularity (plays are included which, in their original form, go back as far as 1828, but the great bulk of the plays represented date from the 1860s to 1874, and it is this decade-and-a-half that will be meant when speaking of "the period of the catalogue").

What is even more significant is that, for this era that was too early for on-stage photography (which began tentatively in 1883), these poster cuts show us how the productions looked. Nineteenth-century plays (especially melodramas) tended to be less talky than twentieth-century pieces and to rely much more heavily on the settings and on sensational effects. Comparison of dozens of play texts with these catalogue pictures shows that the anonymous artists were generally very faithful in reproducing the decor and the groupings of characters called for by the author.

An outstanding example is the illustration of Act IV, Scene 1, of the 1857 play *The Poor of New York* (No. 21). The setting is a wintry evening at the southeast corner of Union Square (then still behind a railing) with the 1856 statue of George Washington (since moved inside the park), just a bit west of the Academy of Music (which itself had opened only in 1854) on 14th Street. The indigent Puffy is seen with his hot chestnuts for sale. He, his wife and their son Dan are eating the supper she has prepared, using as a table the trunk which Dan has just been carrying as a porter. Paul Fairweather, whose family have been defrauded of their money by the banker Bloodgood, crouches listlessly in the corner. Badger, the ex-bank clerk whose impulses shift from evil to good, is now poor himself and is selling librettos to wealthy people on their way to the opera at the Academy. Thus, a specific moment of the play is crystallized

TOP TO BOTTOM: *Lydia Thompson, who popularized British burlesque in America; Adah Isaacs Menken, who revitalized the role of Mazeppa; and William J. Florence, star of burlesque, Irish plays and high comedy.*

most circumstantially; and this is far from being an isolated example. (A few cases of imperfect matching of play text and poster cut are mentioned in the Additional Comments.) In most cases, as was only natural for advertising purposes, the moment captured was either an act climax, a nodal point of the plot, or—with decided predilection—a "sensation": a fire, explosion, avalanche, shipwreck or other disaster.

In view of the frequency of blazes and billows, it may be of interest to see how these effects could be produced at the time. An 1886 source (*Theatrical and Circus Life*, by John J. Jennings, Hebert & Cole Publishing Co., St. Louis)—later than the period of the catalogue but still applicable—thus describes the preparation of the fire scene in *The Poor of New York* (illustration No. 23):

> The scene painter gets up his house in three pieces. The roof is swung from the "flies"; the front wall is in two pieces, a jagged line running from near the top of one side of the scene to the lower end of the other side.

The shutters that are to fall

> are fastened to the scene with "quick match," a preparation of powder, alcohol, and lamp wick. Iron window and door frames are covered with oakum soaked in alcohol or other fire-quickening fluid. Steam is made to represent smoke, and the steam itself is obtained by dissolving lime in water. A platform from the side affords a footing to the firemen who are fighting the flames in the very midst of the burning building, and an endless towel with painted flames keeps moving across the picture after the first wall and roof have been allowed to fall in, while red fire plays upon the whole picture and "flash torches" are made to represent leaping tongues of flame.

From the same work:

> There are two ways of producing ocean waves. Sometimes a piece of blue cloth with dashes of white paint for wave-crests covers the entire stage, when the necessary motion of the waters is obtained by having men or boys stationed in the entrances to sway the sea. Again, each billow may be made to show separate with the alternate rows of billows rearing their white crests between the tips of the row on each side. These billows are rocked backward and forward—to and from the audience—while the ocean's roar comes from a wooden box lined with tin and containing a small quantity of bird shot.

That these expedients did not always satisfy every member of every audience is shown by a review of the play *Surf* (see illustration No. 143) in the weekly magazine *Spirit of the Times* (Jan. 15, 1870, issue):

> The setting of the piece was marred by the attempt, which has always proved a failure, and never more absolutely than in this instance, to represent by the usual stage appliances the peculiar beauty of dashing water. The surf scene, which was handsomely painted, was thus robbed of its illusion by the clumsy putting of a piece of sail cloth across the stage heavily loaded with white cotton to represent surf.

ABOVE: *F. C. Burnand, editor of "Punch" and author of numerous comic plays, including "Ixion."* BELOW: *Augustin Daly, playwright and foremost American theatrical manager of the late nineteenth century.*

And this was not in a penny-pinching production by barnstormers, but at Augustin Daly's Fifth Avenue Theatre! Furthermore, books of theatrical reminiscences abound in anecdotes of ludicrous breakdowns of stage machinery. But things seem to have worked well enough most of the time.

Sometimes the catalogue illustrations will depict an exterior more naturalistically than it could have appeared to an audience, but anyone familiar with the stagecraft of the day can usually distinguish in the cuts the roles played by backdrops, wings, borders, flats moving in grooves, and constructed elements in the composition of the stage pictures.

The visual impulse to playwrights was so strong in this period that a number of plays were suggested by or built around celebrated contemporary paintings. Illustration No. 30, *Jeanie Deans*, is based on the painting "The Trial of Effie Deans," also called "The Doom," by Robert Scott Lauder, from, in turn, Scott's *Heart of Midlothian*; *Ours* (No. 55) was suggested by John Everett Millais' "The Black Brunswicker"; the last scene of *The Great City* (No. 84) reconstituted "The Railway Station" by William Powell Frith; and the scene depicted in No. 92, *Waiting for the Verdict*, reenacted Abraham Solomon's painting of that name.

Cuts from the catalogue which I have seen used in theatrical printing of the period include the scene from *The Mendicant* (No. 142)—on an 1872 playbill of DeBar's Opera House in St. Louis, featuring Lucille Western in the play—and all three scenes from *Jack and Gill Went Up the Hill* (Nos. 171–173)—used in Fox's souvenir booklet for his original 1866 New York production. Other cuts have appeared sporadically in American and English books and magazines without any source credit. The June 1931 issue of *Theatre Arts* reproduces a copy of the dodger (small handbill) for *The Lottery of Life* (No. 107), with the name of Wallack's Theatre (original production) printed in the available center space.

In order to evaluate the system of organization adopted here, it is necessary to recall the overwhelming influence that the English stage still exerted on the American in this period (only ten years later was there a better balance in favor of native-born playwrights, a trend never since reversed).

Even adaptations into English of Continental plays, chiefly French, came to America via England, although some were made here. These ranged from straight translations to complete overhaulings; credit to the European authors was rarely given. For the purposes of organizing this book, the writer of the English play text has been considered to be the playwright, as he was, in fact, considered by the audience of the period, when they bothered about authors at all.

The basic division of the material is: straight plays (not counting the fact that they may have contained a few songs for relief; incidental music was almost always used), Nos. 1–157; musical pieces, variety and circus, Nos. 158–215; and a miscellany,

ABOVE: *Dion Boucicault, nineteenth-century dramatist par excellence, author of 19 of the plays in this volume.* BELOW: *H. J. Byron, prolific English author of melodrama, farce and burlesque.*

TOP: *John Brougham, actor and author of serious and comic plays.* CENTER: *Olive Logan, playwright and lecturer, author of "Surf."* BOTTOM LEFT: *Tom Taylor, author of "Our American Cousin" and "The Ticket-of-Leave Man."* BOTTOM RIGHT: *Tom Robertson, who changed the course of Anglo-American playwrighting with his quiet domestic dramas.*

Nos. 216–268.

The straight plays are divided into: works by various authors, both English and American, dating from the 1820s through the 1850s, that is, before the basic period of the catalogue (1860s and early 1870s), though obviously still performed in 1875 (Nos. 1–17); plays by major British authors (with separate sections on Boucicault, Taylor, Robertson, Gilbert, Collins, H. J. Byron, Phillips, Halliday, Hazlewood, Falconer; Nos. 18–100); miscellaneous English plays (Nos. 101–106); plays by major American authors (sections on Brougham and Daly; Nos. 107–125); and miscellaneous works either clearly or presumably by American authors (Nos. 126–157).

The musical shows and variety pieces are classed as: ballet extravaganzas (Nos. 158–168); French operettas (Nos. 169 and 170); clown pantomimes (Nos. 171–186); burlesques (Nos. 187–199); other musical entertainments (Nos. 200–206); and variety and circus (Nos. 207–215).

The miscellany includes: stage types (Nos. 216–227); personalities (Nos. 228–237); and assorted graphics (Nos. 238–268).

Only a few brief and isolated comments can be given here on this wealth of material.

A large proportion of the straight plays represented are classic melodramas. At this stage in the development of that fascinating genre, the heroine was not always strictly unsullied, but she was still much put upon by society or by relentless and enterprising villains (sometimes a man was the chief victim), and there was often a pointed contrast between great riches and dire poverty in big cities; as we have seen, natural and man-made cataclysms generally provided "sensations."

The plays of the 1820s through the 1850s include the hardy perennials *Uncle Tom's Cabin* (Nos. 10–12) and *Camille* (No. 14).

It is both illuminating and fitting that the man with the greatest single number of plays in the catalogue (Nos. 18–48) should be DION BOUCICAULT, surely the most representative English-language playwright of the century (as well as a stirring actor and an outstanding director) some of whose works are still revived (*London Assurance, The Poor of New York, The Octoroon*). His great range of subject matter and his innovations of all sorts have not yet been given their full due by historians, though his achievement as the creator of the high comedy of rural Irish life has been recognized. His name is also connected with the beginnings of theatrical copyright legislation, royalties for playwrights and touring companies of metropolitan successes, and with improvements in theater fireproofing.

TOM TAYLOR (Nos. 49–54), who wrote both worthy costume drama and insightful plays about contemporary bohemians, criminals and detectives, is best remembered for *Our American Cousin* (No. 49) and *The Ticket-of-Leave Man* (No. 50).

TOM ROBERTSON (Nos. 55–64), whose best works were originally produced by the Bancrofts at the Prince of Wales's Theatre in London, is noted both as the creator of a more natural kind of tragicomedy about everyday people—his works of this type, with their then unusual one-word titles, are generally regarded as a turning-point in the development of the English drama—and as a pioneer in the then all but unknown art of stage direction.

The career of W. S. GILBERT (Nos. 65 and 66) included much more—including a great deal of sterling worth—than his fine operettas in association with Arthur Sullivan.

WILKIE COLLINS (Nos. 67 and 68) was primarily a novelist, but dramatized some of his own books.

HENRY JAMES BYRON (Nos. 69–76), associated with Mrs. Bancroft (then still Marie Wilton) at the outset of her venture at the Prince of Wales's, was a prolific author of comedy and melodrama, though he is perhaps best remembered for his pun-filled burlesques (see Nos. 188 and 190).

WATTS PHILLIPS (Nos. 77–83) wrote historical plays and solidly constructed melodramas, the original casts of which were filled with illustrious names.

ANDREW HALLIDAY (Nos. 84–89) was an expert at dramatizing famous novels, and his plays of contemporary London life must have had an authentic ring, since he was the author of the section on beggars in Henry Mayhew's documentary study *London Labour and the London Poor*.

The plays of COLIN HENRY HAZLEWOOD (Nos. 90–94) are not nearly as good as those of the preceding writers, but he suited the less demanding sensation-seekers of the day.

EDMUND FALCONER (Nos. 95–100), who also worked in America, specialized in Irish subjects. The popularity of such plays in New York and other American cities is readily understandable, the large Irish-American population being actively sympathetic to the Fenian agitation then occurring in the homeland.

JOHN BROUGHAM, actor and playwright (Nos. 107–109), was Irish-born, but did most of his work in New York, where he unsuccessfully managed several theaters. He is also represented in the section on burlesque (No. 192).

AUGUSTIN DALY (Nos. 110–125) made a reputation as a playwright before becoming world-famous as one of the most conscientious managers in New York, where his stock company was a training ground for stars. He continued to adapt Continental plays, especially German ones, throughout his career.

The section of miscellaneous American plays includes an adaptation (No. 126) co-authored by another great New York manager (and romantic actor), Lester Wallack; an early success of Bartley Campbell (Nos. 150 and 151), whose work became important in expanding the opportunities for American playwrights; and two of the most popular melodramas of the nineteenth century, performed well into the twentieth: *East Lynne*

TOP TO BOTTOM: *Exterior of the Union Square Theatre in New York during the original run of "The Two Orphans"; Wallack's Theatre at Broadway and 13th Street (managed by Lester Wallack from 1861 to 1881); and a typical theater interior of the early 1880s.*

The American first-run portrayers of the title roles in "The Two Orphans." ABOVE: Kate Claxton as the blind girl Louise. BELOW: Kitty Blanchard as her sister Henriette.

(Nos. 128–130) and *The Two Orphans* (Nos. 152–155).

Though for convenience included in this section, *Maria Antonietta* (No. 157) is actually an example of the many foreign works then performed by visiting stars in their own language; in this case, Adelaide Ristori played Giacometti's work in Italian, and the world première was in New York.

The BALLET EXTRAVAGANZA (Nos. 158–168), already of many decades' standing in Europe, burst upon the consciousness of New Yorkers with *The Black Crook* in 1866. There was an acted story in these shows, but the ballet interludes and, as time went by, more and more variety acts of all sorts, were the main thing. These pieces should not be thought of as mere leg shows, since some of the dancers were to rise to the top of their profession; one need only mention Rita Sangalli of the original *Black Crook* company, who later at the Paris Opéra created the title roles of *Sylvia* by Delibes and *Namouna* by Lalo.

FRENCH OPERETTA, as codified by Offenbach (Nos. 169 and 170), was imported to New York, in French, by H. L. Bateman. Soon, however, Bateman relinquished his rights in this genre to Jim Fisk, who was opening his famous Grand Opera House.

Unlike nineteenth-century French pantomime (unforgettably recreated in the film *Les enfants du paradis*), English CLOWN PANTOMIME is not a wordless show, though equally derived from Italian *commedia dell'arte*. Basically a children's Christmas entertainment, clown pantomime (Nos. 171–186) is based loosely on nursery rhymes and tales, and embodies much variety entertainment (though this was not always so). George L. Fox was not the only American star Clown, but by far the most illustrious, and his pantomime *Humpty Dumpty* had one of the longest runs of any New York show in the nineteenth century.

The BURLESQUE of this period (Nos. 187–199), while it seemed spicy to many Americans, was not yet the bump and grind of the twentieth century. An English import, like so many other types of entertainment, the burlesque was a short spoof on an opera, fairy tale or event from history or mythology, with spoken text in rhyming couplets and songs consisting of new words set (almost always) to existing well-known tunes, either standards or current music-hall hits.* There were always a few male characters played by women in tights. New York had seen burlesques before (Brougham had written some excellent original ones in the 1850s, and by 1866 the Worrells and William J. Florence were presenting the latest English variety), but it was the arrival of the actress-singer-dancer-manager Lydia Thompson and her company of "British Blondes" in 1868 that made New York and other American cities literally burlesque-mad.

* Some of the English songs introduced to America in the late 1860s by burlesque performers and variety artists like the Lingards included "The Flying Trapeze," "Champagne Charlie Is My Name," "Captain Jinks of the Horse Marines" and "Walking Down Broadway" (a rewrite of the English "Walking in the Zoo"; this seems never to have been pointed out before by Sigmund Spaeth or other song sleuths who have written about "Walking Down Broadway").

The coverage of extravaganza and burlesque in the catalogue is quite extensive. Perhaps there was a special interest in this type of show in Philadelphia, which was a center of manufacturing "symmetricals," padded tights (skinniness was not in favor) that could also palliate such defects as knock-knees or bowlegs.

The posters concerned with VARIETY (forerunner of vaudeville) include one for a sketch (No. 201) that was performed by Harrigan and Hart, soon to become famous for their musical plays about New York minority groups. Although the circus is mentioned prominently in the title of the catalogue, there is relatively little material about it, although the circus was already a great power in the American entertainment industry (huge combines were already a major factor in the circus world, and by 1870 Barnum was beginning to enter various circus partnerships).

The material included here in the "miscellaneous" section is just a small portion of what the catalogue contains in this regard, since I have been more interested in specific plays and shows.

The captions on the picture pages give: the full title of the play; the year in which it was first performed (generally, in London and New York for English plays, in New York only for American plays; occasionally, an important première, or at least earlier performance, in another city is indicated); where applicable or known, the source of the play (foreign play, novel, etc.); and, wherever possible, an identification of the specific moment in the action that is illustrated, with indication of act and scene.

The Additional Comments which follow the illustrations contain a variety of data that could not be contained in the captions.

The Alphabetical Lists, of Playwrights and of Plays, include the authors and titles of the foreign-language works cited as sources of the English-language plays.

Other principals of the first New York run of "The Two Orphans." LEFT TO RIGHT: *F. F. Mackay as the poor Pierre; McKee Rankin as his criminal brother Jacques; Marie Wilkins as their mother, the hag La Frochard; and Charles R. Thorne, Jr., as the Chevalier Maurice de Vaudrey.*

OLD-TIME WOODCUTS
From the Nineteenth-Century Stage

1. THE RED ROVER (from James Fenimore Cooper's novel; first dramatization by Samuel H. Chapman, Philadelphia, 1828). End of the play: the pirate ship is destroyed. 2. THE ICE WITCH; OR, THE FROZEN HAND, by John Baldwin Buckstone (London, 1831; N.Y., 1832). Act I, Scene 5: the coast of Norway; the witch Druda (left) transforms a rock into a golden galley so that the man she has enthralled—Harold, the Sea King—and his servant, Magnus Snoro, can return home.

MAZEPPA; OR, THE WILD HORSE OF TARTARY, by Henry M. Milner (from Byron's poem; London, 1831; N.Y., 1833). 3. Act II, Scene 1: Mazeppa, tied to a wild horse for presuming to love a Polish noblewoman, is borne through the Dnieper region. 4. Act II, Scene 6: Recognized as prince of the Tartars, he leads a retaliatory force against Poland.

5. The French Spy; or, The Siege of Constantina, by John Thomas Haines (London, 1831; N.Y., 1832). Act II, Scene 3: in the prison of an Algerian fortress, Matilde de Marique, disguised as an Arab boy, grapples with the wily native Mohammed. 6. The People's Lawyer, by Joseph Stevens Jones (Boston, 1839). The chief comic character: the blundering Yankee farmer Solon Shingle.

7. CAPTAIN KYD; OR, THE WIZARD OF THE SEA, by Joseph Stevens Jones (Boston, 1839). Act II, Scene 5: the hut of the witch Elpsy at Hell Gate, Manhattan, 1699; Elpsy summons up the fiend Cusha to prepare a magic amulet for the pirate Kyd; in the background, visions of a British ship that will attack Kyd, and of a hanged pirate. 8. NICK OF THE WOODS, by Louisa H. Medina (N.Y., 1838; from Robert Montgomery Bird's novel). Act II, Scene 5: Nick, the Avenger, scares off hostile Indians by shooting the falls in a blazing canoe.

9. THE GREEN BUSHES; OR, A HUNDRED YEARS AGO, by John Baldwin Buckstone (London and N.Y., 1845). Act II: the Mississippi valley in 1747; the heroine Miami (daughter of a Frenchman and an Indian), who has married the exiled Irish rebel Connor O'Kennedy.

UNCLE TOM'S CABIN; OR, LIFE AMONG THE LOWLY, by George L. Aiken (from Harriet Beecher Stowe's novel; Troy, N.Y., 1852). 10. Uncle Tom. 11. Topsy. 12. Act III, Scene 2: St. Clare's plantation; little Eva reads aloud from the Bible and Tom explains the passage.

13. THE SEA OF ICE; OR, THE PRAYER OF THE WRECKED, AND THE GOLD-SEEKER OF MEXICO (London, 1853; N.Y., 1854; adapted from *La prière des naufragés*, 1853, by Adolphe D'Ennery and Ferdinand Dugué). Act II: set adrift by mutineers, Marie, daughter of Captain de Lascours, says the prayer her mother has taught her. 14. CAMILLE; OR, THE FATE OF A COQUETTE (N.Y., 1853; adapted from *La dame aux camélias*, 1852, by Alexandre Dumas *fils*). Act IV: Armand Duval, believing Camille has left him voluntarily for a richer man, repays his debt to her in an insulting manner.

THE THREE FAST MEN, AND THE FEMALE ROBINSON CRUSOES, by W. B. English (N.Y., 1858; earlier in Boston). 15. Belcher Que, the sporting man. 16. Mungo Jim, the chimney sweep. 17. A masquerade ball. "Fast men" meant playboys, or high livers.

THE CORSICAN BROTHERS (London and N.Y., 1852; adapted by Boucicault from *Les frères corses*, 1850, after Dumas *père*, by Eugène Grangé and Xavier de Montépin). Act III: the Forest of Fontainebleau. 18. In a duel, Fabien dei Franchi kills Château-Renaud, slayer of his twin brother Louis. 19. The ghost of Louis appears to Fabien, now that his death is avenged.

20. FAUST AND MARGUERITE (London, 1854; N.Y., 1857?; adapted from Michel Carré's *Faust et Marguerite*, 1850). Act I or III: Mephistopheles, Faust and Marguerite outside the church. 21. THE POOR OF NEW YORK (N.Y., 1857; adapted from *Les pauvres de Paris*, 1856, by Edouard Brisebarre and Eugène Nus). Act IV, Scene 1: Union Square; on a cold night, various characters vend chestnuts or opera librettos, or merely suffer passively. See Introduction, page ix, for a description of this scene.

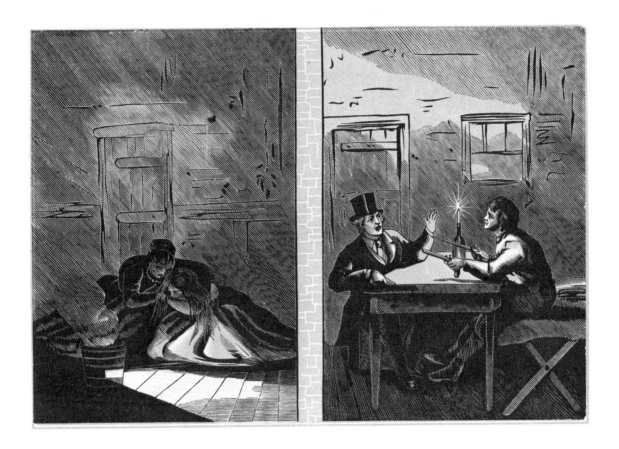

THE POOR OF NEW YORK. 22. Act IV, Scene 3: adjoining rooms in a Five Points garret; Badger holds the grasping banker Bloodgood at bay, while Mrs. Fairweather and her daughter Lucy, whom Bloodgood has impoverished, attempt to commit suicide by inhaling charcoal fumes. 23. Act V, Scene 2: exterior of the same building, which Bloodgood has set on fire to destroy incriminating papers hidden there. For fire effects, see Introduction, page x.

24. PAUVRETTE; OR, UNDER THE SNOW (N.Y., 1858; adapted from *La bergère des Alpes*, 1852, by Adolphe D'Ennery and Charles Desnoyer). Act III: the "summit of the Alps"; an avalanche cuts off retreat so that Count Maurice de Grandval must spend the winter in the hut of Pauvrette, the mysterious Alpine girl.

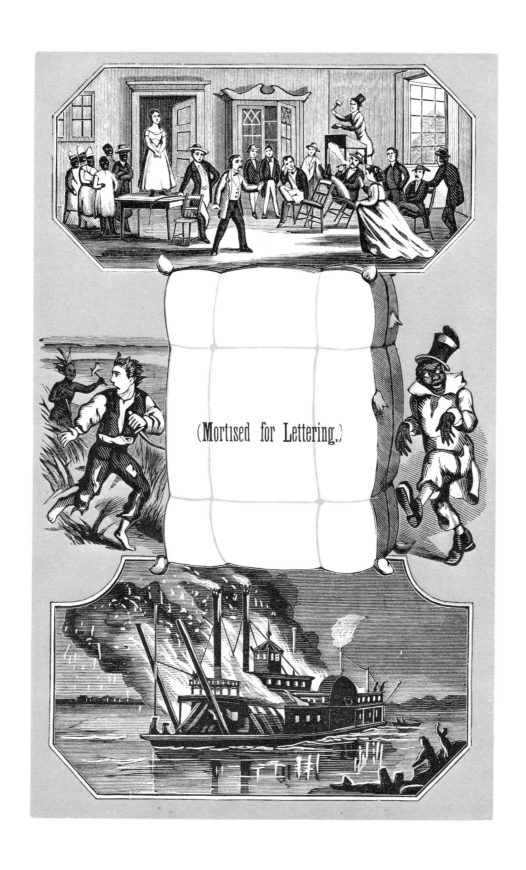

(Mortised for Lettering.)

25. THE OCTOROON; OR, LIFE IN LOUISIANA (N.Y., 1859; suggested by Mayne Reid's novel *The Quadroon*). Scenes shown are: (top) Act III, room in Mrs. Peyton's house, where the octoroon girl Zoe is put up for auction; (bottom) Act IV, the wharf, with the steamboat *Magnolia* set afire by the convict M'Closky; and (left) Act V, Scene 3, a cedar swamp, in which the Indian Wahnotee pursues M'Closky, who has killed his friend, little Paul (shown, probably, at right center).

THE COLLEEN BAWN; OR, THE BRIDES OF GARRYOWEN (N.Y., 1860; based on Gerald Griffin's novel *The Collegians*). Two moments from Act II, Scene 6, the "Devil's Pool." 26. Danny Mann tries to drown Eily O'Connor in order to remove all record of the peasant girl's secret marriage to his master. 27. The vagabond Myles-na-Coppaleen, who is in love with Eily, saves her.

ARRAH-NA-POGUE; OR, THE WICKLOW WEDDING (Dublin, 1864; London and N.Y., 1865). Two moments from Act III, Scene 3, the prison in which Shaun-the-Post, courageously shielding an Irish rebel (it is 1798), has been confined. 28. Shaun breaks out of his cell and scales the ivy-covered wall. 29. He arrives at the top in time to save his sweetheart Arrah from the double-dealing Michael Feeney.

30. JEANIE DEANS; OR, THE HEART OF MIDLOTHIAN (N.Y., 1860; from Sir Walter Scott's novel). Act II, Scene 3: Jeanie and her fiancé Reuben Butler comfort her father David, who has fainted upon hearing his younger daughter Effie found guilty of child murder. 31. RIP VAN WINKLE (London and N.Y., 1865; based on Washington Irving's story and various early dramatizations). Act II: the kitchen of Rip's cottage; his shrewish wife Gretchen drives him out into the storm as their daughter Meenie weeps and the innkeeper's son, Hendrick Vedder, looks on.

RIP VAN WINKLE. 32. Act III: in the mountains, Rip meets the ghosts of Henry Hudson's crew, who invite him to drink from their keg. 33. Act IV, Scene 3: the village of Falling Waters twenty years later; Rip is not recognized (the inn sign now portrays George Washington instead of George III).

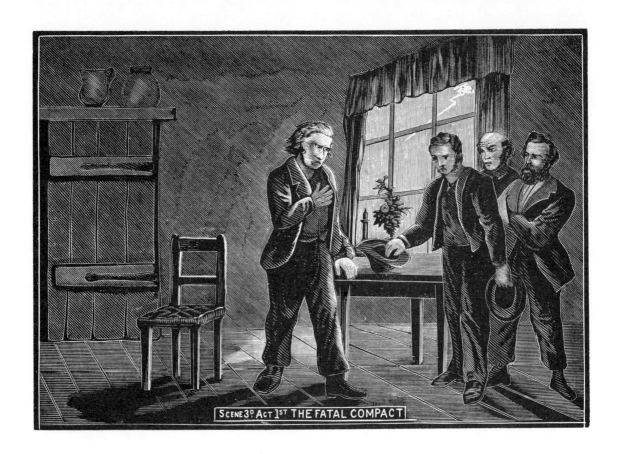

SCENE 3D ACT 1ST THE FATAL COMPACT

THE LONG STRIKE (London and N.Y., 1866). 34. Act I, Scene 3: the Manchester home of the striking workman Noah Learoyd, who draws the fatal lot from the hat: he must burn Richard Readley's mill. 35. Act II, Scene 3: Fuller's Lane, outside Readley's house; Readley is shot by Noah from behind the hedge while keeping an assignation with Noah's wife Jane.

36. HUNTED DOWN; OR, THE TWO LIVES OF MARY LEIGH (London, 1866; N.Y., 1869). Act I: London home of the painter John Leigh; Mary has fainted at the arrival of Rawdon Scudamore, her first husband, who had abandoned her and whom she believed dead; her husband's model Clara (actually Scudamore's legal wife) looks on. 37.

FLYING SCUD; OR, A FOUR-LEGGED FORTUNE (London, 1866; N.Y., 1867). Act II, Scene 4: the beach at Calais, where a duel has been fought between the sharper Captain Goodge and—apparently his gambling victim, Lord Cecil Woodbie—but in reality Julia Latimer, niece of another sharper, and in love with Cecil; she is wounded.

38. AFTER DARK; A TALE OF LONDON LIFE (London and N.Y., 1868; adapted from *Les Bohémiens de Paris*, 1843, by Adolphe D'Ennery and Eugène Grangé). Act I, Scene 6: an arch of Blackfriars Bridge, with the Thames and St. Paul's; Eliza (really Fanny Dalton), whose life has been manipulated by criminals, tries to end it all.

FORMOSA; OR, THE RAILROAD TO RUIN (London and N.Y., 1869). 39. Act II, Scene 3: the courtesan Formosa's villa at Fulham, where the Oxford rower Tom Burroughs is induced to dally and gamble. 40. Act IV, Scene 5: the Thames at Barnes Bridge, showing the boat race between Oxford and Cambridge.

LOST AT SEA; A LONDON STORY (written in collaboration with Henry James Byron; London, 1869; N.Y., 1870). **41.** Act II, Scene 4: Hungerford Bridge and the Thames, with a steamboat pier in the foreground. **42.** Act III, Scene 7: the garret home of the herbalist Jessop in Love Lane, Lambeth; Jessop's daughter Katey saves the rich merchant Walter Coram (supposed lost at sea), whom her father has been impersonating, from the fire intended to get him out of the way forever.

43. FOUL PLAY (written in collaboration with Charles Reade; London and N.Y., 1868; based on Reade's novel, which was suggested by the play *Le portefeuille rouge*, 1862, by Narcisse Fournier and Henri-Horace Meyer). Act II: a Pacific island; Helen Rolleston prevents Hazel (actually Robert Penfold), whom she has come to love, from signaling to a ship because that means of rescuing her would send him back to his undeserved imprisonment. 44. THE RAPPAREE; OR, THE TREATY OF LIMERICK (London and N.Y., 1870). Act II, Scene 3: a room in Mona Castle, home of Roderick O'Malley, who has had a fire set to escape a trap laid for him by the soldiers of William of Orange; he saves Grace O'Hara by an exterior spiral staircase seen through a breach in the wall.

ELFIE; OR, THE CHERRY-TREE INN (Glasgow, London, and N.Y., 1871). 45. Act I, Scene 3: exterior of the inn; Rose Aircastle thanks Sedley Deepcar for offering to pay her father's debt to the innkeeper Sam Filey. 46. Act II, Scene 2: a woodland lane; Deepcar looks on as the blind sailor Joe punishes the peddler Sadlove for molesting Elfie, the servant of the inn.

BELLE LAMAR (N.Y., 1874). 47. Poster establishing the play's Civil War setting. 48. Act III: the Whitestone Gap; Belle, a Southern spy, is now in the custody of her husband, the Northern colonel Philip Bligh; the Union camp is hopelessly ringed by Confederate forces.

49. OUR AMERICAN COUSIN, by Taylor (N.Y., 1858). Shown are three characters: Lord Dundreary (center), probably the butler Binny (left) and the Yankee cousin Asa Trenchard (right). This is the play President Lincoln was viewing when he was assassinated.

50. THE TICKET-OF-LEAVE MAN (London and N.Y., 1863; based on *Léonard* [or *Le retour de Melun*], 1862, by Edouard Brisebarre and Eugène Nus). Act IV, Scene 1: the Bridgewater Arms coffee room; the detective Hawkshaw reveals his identity to the ill-fated ticket-of-leave man (parolee) Bob Brierly, who has written a warning note to the bill-broker whose office he is being forced to rob.

51. HENRY DUNBAR; OR, A DAUGHTER'S TRIAL (London, 1865; N.Y., 1866; from the novel by Mary Elizabeth Braddon). Act III: a room in Maudsley Abbey; Margaret Wentworth discovers that the rich banker Henry Dunbar, whom she has been seeking, has been killed by her own father, who is now impersonating him.

52. MARY WARNER; OR, TRIED IN THE FIRE (London and N.Y., 1869). Act IV, Scene 4: Mary, who went to jail for theft in place of her husband (he was also innocent), is finally reunited with her daughter, little Mary, on the child's seventh birthday. 53. 'TWIXT AXE AND CROWN; OR, THE LADY ELIZABETH (London and N.Y., 1870; adapted from *Elizabeth Prinzessin von England*, by Charlotte Birch-Pfeiffer). Act III, Scene 2: the lieutenant's garden in the Tower of London; on his way to execution, Sir Thomas Wyatt is allowed to greet the prisoner Edward Courtenay, Earl of Devonshire, in hopes that he will implicate Courtenay and Princess Elizabeth in political crimes.

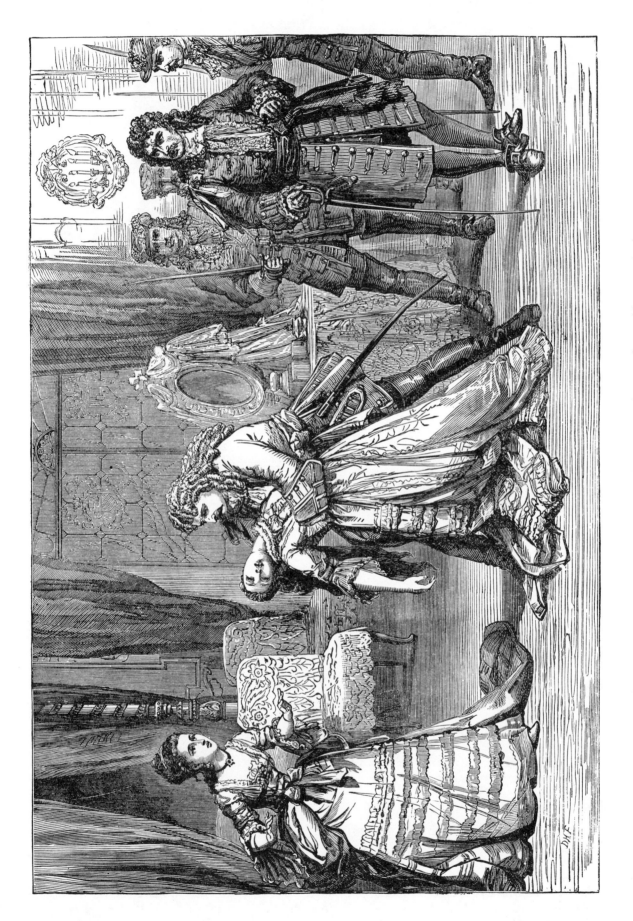

54. LADY CLANCARTY; OR, WEDDED AND WOOED (London, 1874; Brooklyn, 1875). Act III: Lady Clancarty's bedchamber in her father's London home, 1696; she faints as her Jacobite husband is arrested as a traitor; looking on are her friend Lady Betty Noel and her heartless brother Lord Charles Spencer.

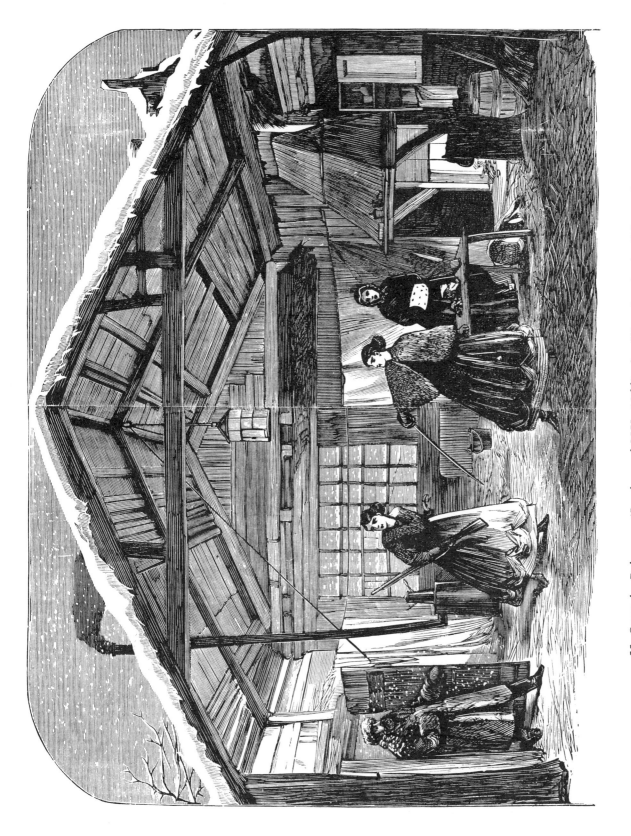

55. OURS, by Roberston (London and N.Y., 1866). Act III: a hut in the Crimea; the Englishwomen Mary Netley, Blanche Haye and Lady Shendryn are visiting the front; the Russian Prince Petrovski, formerly engaged to Blanche, enters as a prisoner of war. See Introduction.

56. CASTE (London and N.Y., 1867). Act III: the little Eccles home in Stangate; the haughty Marquise de St. Maur offers money to her (apparently) widowed daughter-in-law, Esther Eccles D'Alroy, if Esther will part with her child; looking on are Esther's worthless father and her sister Polly.

PROGRESS (London and N.Y., 1869; adapted from *Les ganaches*, 1862, by Victorien Sardou). **57.** Act I: a drawing room in Mompesson Abbey; the snooping spinster Miss Myrnie watches the happy meeting of the progressive young engineer John Ferne and the ailing family ward Eva Sum-mers. **58.** Act II: the tapestry chamber in the Abbey; Eva, falsely informed that Ferne avowed love to her merely out of pity, has deliberately courted death by walking out into the snow.

DREAMS (Liverpool, London and N.Y., 1869; suggested by Alfred Tennyson's poem "Lady Clara Vere de Vere"). 59. Act I: a modest room in Mainz; the German cavalry officer Harfthal consoles his wife (and their ward Caroline Lindeck) as their son Rudolf leaves for England to study musical composition. 60. Act V: the back entrance of a convent; Caroline is about to take the veil when hitherto neglectful Rudolf arrives (with his mother) to make her his bride.

61. SCHOOL (London and N.Y., 1869; adapted from *Aschenbrödel*, by Roderich Benedix). Act I: a wood near a private school, where Arthur Beaufoy and Jack Poyntz, out hunting, meet some adorable schoolgirls as the elderly Percy (Beau) Farintosh looks on.

62. SCHOOL. Act II: a classroom, where the girls, led by Naomi Tighe, revolt against the petty tyranny of the teacher Krux. 63. HOME (London and N.Y., 1869; adapted from *L'aventurière*, 1848, by Emile Augier). Act II: the home of Mr. Dorrison, who is driving out the guest whom he suspects of making love to his intended second wife (an adventuress), when the guest reveals himself to be Dorrison's own son Alfred.

64. HOME. ACT III: now that the adventuress is gone, Dorrison, his son and daughter (Lucy) and their future spouses (Dora Thornhough and Bertie Thompson) all enjoy the contentments of domesticity.

65. PYGMALION AND GALATEA, by Gilbert (London, 1871; N.Y., 1872). Act I: the home of the Greek sculptor Pygmalion, who marvels when his statue Galatea comes to life. 66. THE WICKED WORLD (London and N.Y., 1873).

Act I: Fairyland, where two mortals, Sir Ethais and Sir Phyllon, summoned there by immortals who are curious about love, immediately resume the combat they were engaged in on earth.

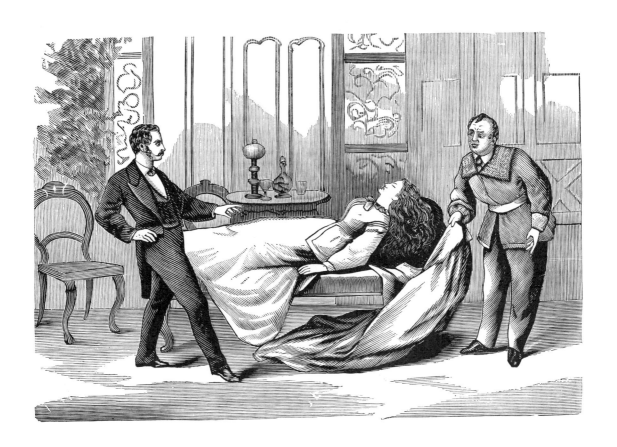

67. THE WOMAN IN WHITE (London, 1871; N.Y., 1873; dramatized by Collins from his own novel). Count Fosco (right) reveals the unconscious woman in white, Anne Catherick, to (probably) Sir Percival Glyde, who is amazed by her resemblance to Lady Glyde, the former Laura Fairlie.

68. THE NEW MAGDALEN (London and N.Y., 1873; from Collins' novel). Prologue: a cottage on the Front in the Franco-Prussian War; the English nurse Mercy Merrick thinks her compatriot Grace Roseberry is killed by a shell coming through the roof.

PLAYS BY WILLIAM WILKIE COLLINS   39

THE LANCASHIRE LASS; OR, TEMPTED, TRIED AND TRUE, by Byron (Liverpool, 1867; London and N.Y., 1868). 69. Prologue, Scene 2: the village home of farmer Kirby; a secret letter from his daughter Ruth to the villainous painter Redburn is intercepted and causes much misunderstanding. 70. Act II, Scene 2: A London wharf, where Redburn falsely accuses Ruth's sweetheart Ned Clayton of murder.

71. THE LANCASHIRE LASS. Act IV: a farmhouse in Australia, to which Ned has been transported; Redburn turns up again to threaten the lives of Ned and Ruth (now Ned's wife). 72. BLOW FOR BLOW (London, 1868; N.Y., 1869). Act III, Scene 3: the third story of a lodging house; base John Drummond is about to manhandle Alice Petherick (who refuses to impersonate her dead twin sister for purposes of blackmail) when one of her well-wishers, Charley Spraggs, knocks Drummond over the balustrade.

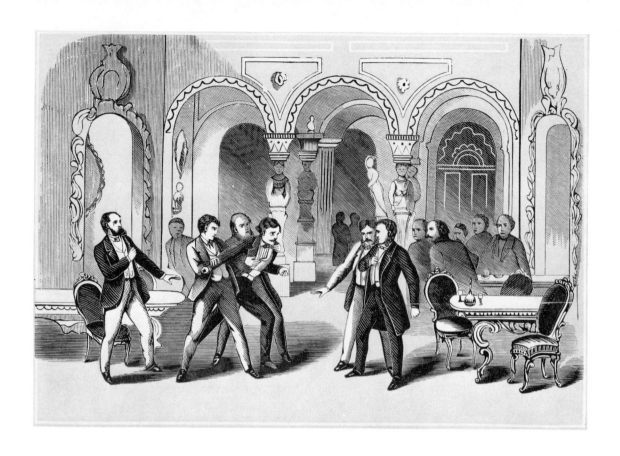

73. CYRIL'S SUCCESS (London, 1868; Brooklyn, 1869). Act IV, Scene 2: the smoking room of the Grantley Club, St. James's; the playwright Cyril Cuthbert is restrained from attacking Major Treherne, who has been too attentive to Mrs. Cuthbert. 74. PARTNERS FOR LIFE (London, 1871; N.Y., 1874). Act II: the drawing room in Horace Mervyn's home; Mervyn and other members of the household are stunned to find cousin Tom Gilroy embracing Fanny Smith (courted by Mervyn, but actually Gilroy's estranged wife).

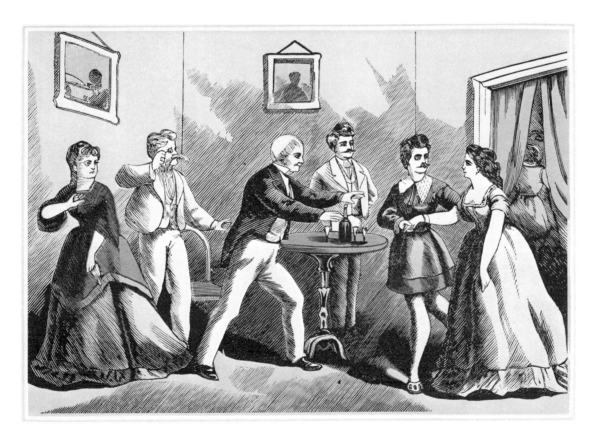

THE PROMPTER'S BOX; A STORY OF THE FOOTLIGHTS AND THE FIRESIDE (London, 1870). **75.** Act I: a provincial boarding house; the banker Sir Michael Glendinning arrives unexpectedly to confront his barrister son Ernest, who is in love with Florence, a prompter's daughter. **76.** Act III, Scene 3: the greenroom of the Royal Polygon Theatre; Florence makes a successful London acting debut in a play by Ernest.

PLAYS BY HENRY JAMES BYRON   43

LOST IN LONDON, by Phillips (N.Y., 1865?; London, 1867). 77. Act I, Scene 3: a coal mine, where the miner Job Armroyd learns that his much younger wife Nelly has run off to London with the owner of the mine. 78. Act II,

Scene 3: outside the Ferns, a Regent's Park villa belonging to Nelly; Job, searching everywhere for his wife, recognizes her at the window.

79. LOST IN LONDON. Act III: a cottage near London; Nelly interposes in a scuffle between her husband and her tempter, Gilbert Featherstone.

NOT GUILTY (London and N.Y., 1869). **80.** Act I: a garret in Southampton, where Robert Arnold is arrested for theft (on a baker's evidence); on the roof is Silas Jarrett, the real culprit, who planted a false clue. **81.** Act III, Scene 3: a battlefield in India ten years later, during the Sepoy Mutiny of 1857.

82. NOBODY'S CHILD (London and N.Y., 1867). Act III, Scene 2: a ravine in Cornwall, where the waif Joe courageously retrieves a lost will and testament as Patty Lavrock, niece of the village innkeeper, holds the rope. **83. ON THE JURY** (London, 1871; N.Y., 1872). Act III, Scene 2: the Thames near London Bridge; the boat which Edith Ferrars has hired, in order to get aboard the Hamburg packet before her persecuted father leaves for Russia, is run down by a steamboat.

84. The Great City, by Halliday (London, 1867). The "Jolly Beggars' Club," with an odd assortment of vagabonds, chimney sweeps and street minstrels.

LITTLE EM'LY (London and N.Y., 1869; from Charles Dickens' novel *David Copperfield*). **85.** Act II, Scene 3: the yard of Canterbury Cathedral; the fallen woman Martha promises David and old Dan'l Peggoty she will find the runaway Emily. **86.** Act III, Scene 3: the seashore at Yarmouth; Emily's rejected lover Ham Peggoty swims out to rescue victims of a wreck—one of whom is Emily's seducer Steerforth.

AMY ROBSART (London, 1870; N.Y., 1872; from Sir Walter Scott's novel *Kenilworth*). 87. Act III, Scene 2: the exterior of Kenilworth Castle, where mummers stage a pageant for Queen Elizabeth. 88. Act IV, Scene 3: the roof of Mervyn's tower, where Sir Richard Varney, who has shot the messenger Mike Lambourne, mistakenly falls through his own drawbridge trap as Amy rushes out of the turret and the Earl of Leicester mounts the stair.

89. NOTRE DAME; OR, THE GIPSY GIRL OF PARIS, by Halliday (London, 1871; N.Y., by 1873; from Victor Hugo's novel *Notre-Dame de Paris*). Act III, Scene 2: the roof of the Cathedral; the hunchback Quasimodo hurls down Archdeacon Claude Frollo as Phoebus and Gudule arrive with a pardon for Esmeralda. 90. THE HOUSE ON THE BRIDGE OF NOTRE DAME, by Hazlewood (London, 1861; N.Y., 1866; adapted by Hazlewood from *La maison du pont de Notre-Dame*, 1860, by Théodore Barrière and Henry de Kock). Act III, Scene 1: the house mentioned in the title, where Mélanie de St. Ange of Martinique, formerly fiancée of the murdered heir to a fortune, is residing.

PLAYS BY ANDREW HALLIDAY AND BY COLIN HENRY HAZLEWOOD 51

WAITING FOR THE VERDICT; OR, FALSELY ACCUSED (London, 1859; N.Y., 1864). 91. Act I, Scene 6: the cottage of Jonathan Roseblade; Jonathan tries to calm his son Jasper (as does Jasper's wife Martha) when Jasper takes a hedge stake with which to chastise the man who has brought trouble upon him. 92. Act II, Scene 4: a lobby in the courthouse, where the Reverend Owen Hylton and the Roseblade family await the verdict in Jasper's trial for murder.

93. LADY AUDLEY'S SECRET (London and N.Y., 1863; from Mary Elizabeth Braddon's novel). Act I: the Lime Tree Walk leading up to Audley House; Lady Audley pushes her first (and legal) husband George Talboys into a well in order to retain her present high position. 94. THE MARRIAGE CERTIFICATE (London and Brooklyn, 1867).

95. Peep o' Day; or, Savourneen Deelish (London, 1861; N.Y., 1862; suggested to Falconer by the *Tales by the O'Hara Family*, by John and Michael Banim). Act II, Scene 2: a pattern (fair) at a holy well in Ireland in the late eighteenth century; seen are the Widow Mahone's tent and English Captain Howard.

96. PEEP O' DAY. Act III, Scene 5: the old quarry in the Foil Dhuiv (Dark Valley); Black Mullins is about to kill cast-off Kate Kavanagh with a spade, when her brother Harry, the rebel leader, arrives to save her.

PLAYS BY EDMUND FALCONER 55

97–98. INNISFALLEN; OR, THE MEN IN THE GAP (London and N.Y., 1870). The English scene painter William Telbin's panorama of the lakes of Killarney was imported for this production.

99. OONAGH; OR, THE LOVERS OF LISNAMONA (London, 1866). 100. THE FIREFLY (N.Y., 1868; from Ouida's novel *Under Two Flags*). One of many stage versions of Ouida's novel.

101. PURE GOLD, by John Westland Marston (London and N.Y., 1863). Act I, Scene 3: a wood near Baden-Baden; Frank Rockford finds his Uncle Langley dying after a duel with the spies and sharpers Rinaldo and De l'Epine (at the far left) while police arrive—and accuse Frank of murder. 102. BROTHER SAM, by John Oxenford, Edward Askew Sothern and John Baldwin Buckstone (London, 1865). Based on a character mentioned in *Our American Cousin.*

TRUE TO THE CORE; A STORY OF THE ARMADA, by Angiolo Robson Slous (London and N.Y., 1866). 103. Act I: Plymouth Hoe on the Devon coast; although Martin Truegold, pilot, innkeeper and beacon guardian, has been drugged at the instigation of the nefarious Jesuit Geoffery Dangerfield (and Martin's bride Mabel has fainted), the beacon is lighted by the wild Gypsy girl Marah. 104. Act III: the reef of Eddystone, on which an invading Spanish ship has been wrecked through Martin's purposely wrong advice.

105–106. HERNE THE HUNTER; OR, THE DEMON OF THE WIZARD'S OAK, by Frederick Marchant (London, 1866; from William Harrison Ainsworth's novel *Windsor Castle*).

Two appearances of the supernatural huntsman in the troubled days of Henry VIII, Anne Boleyn, Catherine of Aragon and Cardinal Wolsey.

OTHER BRITISH PLAYS OF THE 1860s AND 1870s

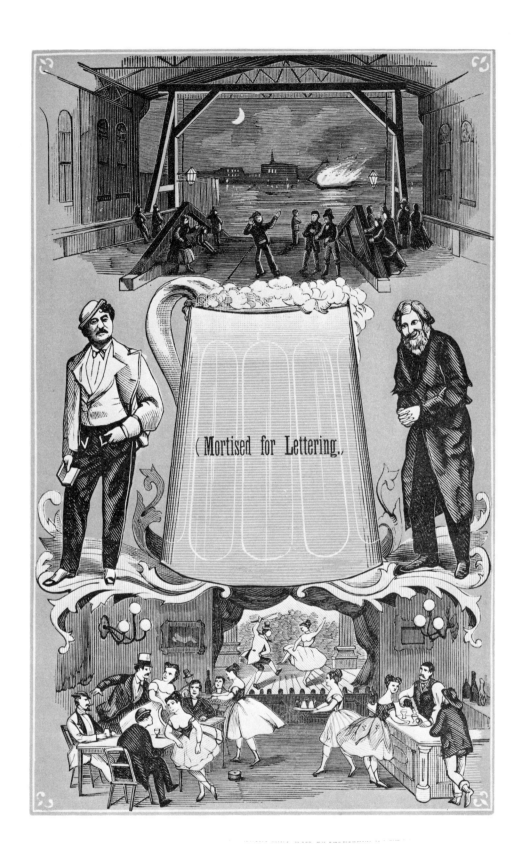

107. THE LOTTERY OF LIFE, by Brougham (N.Y., 1866). Shown are two characters, the "swell" (dandy) Terry O'Halloran and the Fagin-like Mordie Solomons, and two scenes—(bottom) Act II, Scene 3, the interior of the Japonica concert saloon, and (top) Act V, Scene 2, a ferry slip across the East River from Brooklyn Heights, with the yacht *Dashing Spray* set on fire by Solomons.

THE RED LIGHT (N.Y., 1870; from Frederick W. Robinson's novel *Anne Judge, Spinster*). 108. A room in Hugh Aynard's manor house Thirby Cross; the young church organist Edmund Delancy has been badly hurt when investigating the cause of a flashing light in an island boathouse. 109. A poster featuring the light (which is green in the novel!).

110. LEAH, THE FORSAKEN (Boston, 1862; N.Y., 1863; adapted by Daly from *Deborah*, by Salomon Mosenthal). Act IV, Scene 3: a village churchyard in Austria; the Jewess Leah curses Rudolf, son of the local magistrate, who has doubted her loyalty and abandoned her for a Christian bride. 111. GRIFFITH GAUNT; OR, JEALOUSY (N.Y., 1866; from Charles Reade's novel). Act II, Scene 3: the "Dame's Haunt"; Gaunt, jealous of the friendship between his wife Kate and the priest Leonard, bursts into a rage.

GRIFFITH GAUNT. 112. Act III, Scene 3: the pig race at a Lancashire fair, where Gaunt will soon arrive with his new wife. 113. Act IV, Scene 2: the conservatory in Bolton House, Kate Gaunt's home; while Kate seizes a knife in her anger at her husband's bigamy, Gaunt holds the letters that prove her innocence of adultery with Leonard.

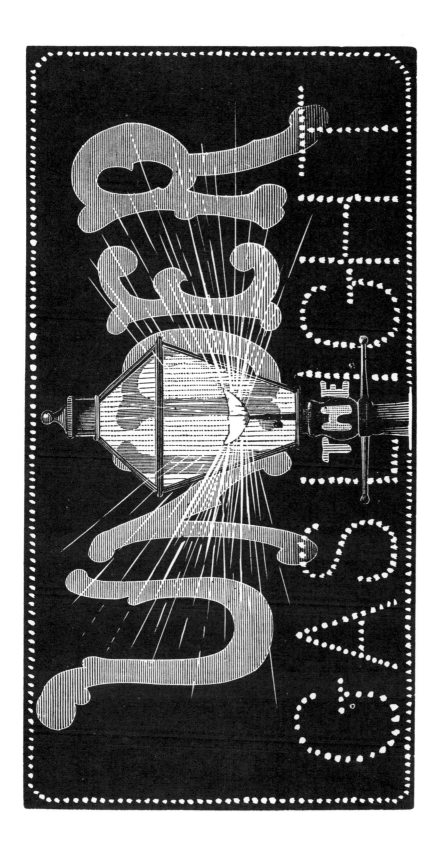

114. UNDER THE GASLIGHT (N.Y., 1867).

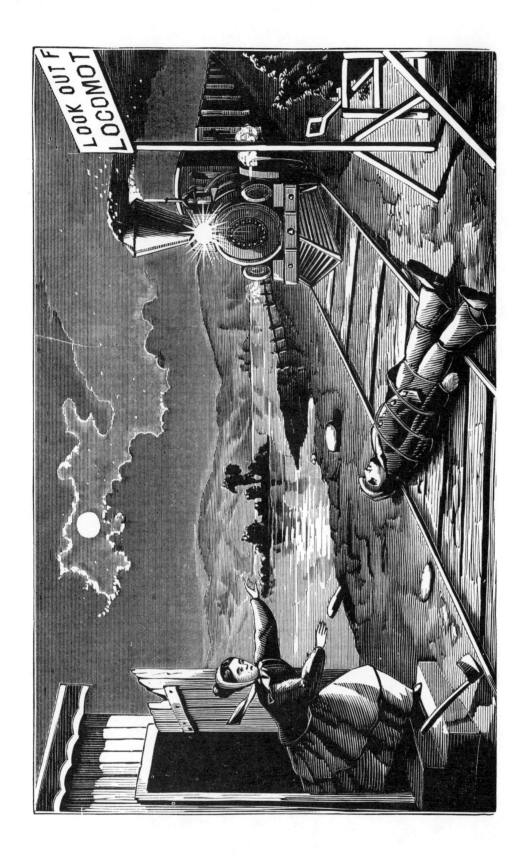

115. UNDER THE GASLIGHT. Act III, Scene 3: a railroad station at Shrewsbury Bend; Laura Courtland, who has been locked in a signalman's shed while awaiting the train, manages to break out in time to save her friend Joe Snorkey from his predicament.

(Mortised for Lettering)

116. A FLASH OF LIGHTNING (N.Y., 1868; partially adapted from *La perle noire*, 1862, by Victorien Sardou). Shown are the lightning flash that causes the heroine Bess Fallon's troubles, and the following scenes: Act II, Scene 3, "Jacob's Ladder," an all-night lodging cellar (Jack Ryver and Bess escape by sliding down the pole of a spiral staircase); Act III, Scene 2, the grand salon of the Hudson River steamer *Daniel Doo* (the evil police detective Skiffley handcuffs Bess outside the staterooms); and Act III, Scene 5 (Jack saves Bess after the boat catches on fire).

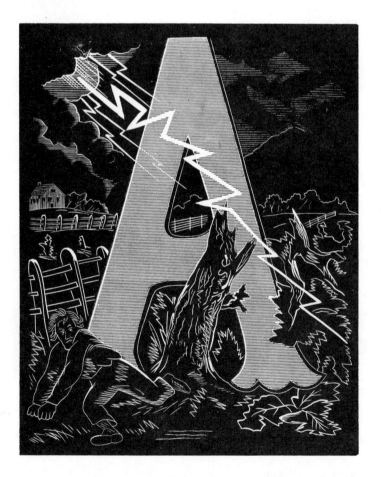

A FLASH OF LIGHTNING. 117. Act III, Scene 3: the steamboat's engine and furnace rooms; Jack tussles with rich
Fred Chauncey, whom he suspects of having stolen Bess's
heart and then deserted her. 118. Another version of the
lightning flash.

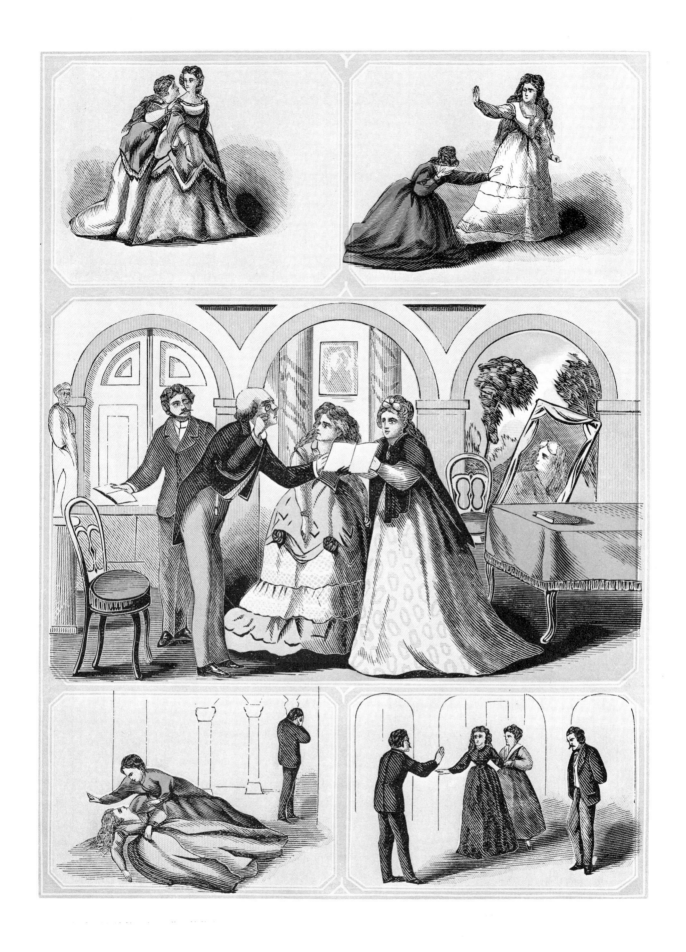

119. FROU-FROU (N.Y., 1870; adapted from the 1869 play by Henri Meilhac and Ludovic Halévy). Center: Act II, a room in Sartorys' home in Paris, where his frivolous wife Gilberte ("Frou-Frou") is rehearsing a charity performance with the Baron and Baroness de Cambri and the Count de Valreas. In the four corners of the poster, Gilberte angrily yields her role as wife and mother to her worthier sister, and returns at last only to die.

FERNANDE (N.Y., 1870; adapted from the 1870 play by Victorien Sardou). 120. Act I: the clandestine gaming establishment of Mme. Sénéchal; kindly Philippe de Pomerol attacks the cynical Roqueville for molesting the proprietress' daughter Fernande. (mother and daughter are at the left, the society woman Clotilde in the center). 121. Act IV: drawing room in the home of André, a Marquis whom Clotilde has tricked into marrying Fernande; now the jealous Clotilde reveals the girl's sordid past.

122–123. DIVORCE (N.Y., 1871; from Anthony Trollope's novel *He Knew He Was Right*). Though the play, about hasty divorces in high society, does have pathetic moments (as depicted in these two posters), it is largely a comedy and ends happily.

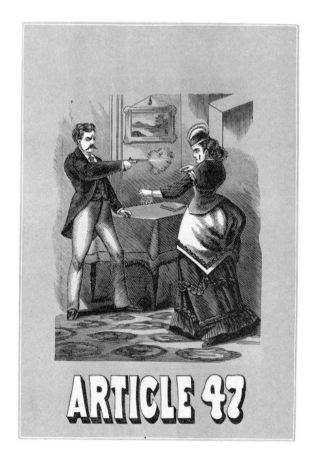

ARTICLE 47 (N.Y., 1872; adapted from *L'Article* 47, 1871, by Adolphe Belot). 124. The half-mad Creole Cora, once shot in the cheek (hence the cloth around her face) by George Duhamel, recognizes the ex-prisoner, who, as George Gerard, has married and is living in Paris illegally. 125. The scene of George shooting Cora.

126. THE ROMANCE OF A POOR YOUNG MAN, by Pierrepont Edwards and Lester Wallack (N.Y., 1860; adapted from *Le roman d'un jeune homme pauvre*, 1858, by Octave Feuillet). Tableau IV: the Tower of Elfen in Brittany; when the poor nobleman Manuel de Champcey is accidentally locked in the ruin with Marguerite Laroque and she fears for her honor, he leaps to the ground. 127. FANCHON, THE CRICKET, by August Waldauer (N.Y., 1862; adapted from *Die Grille*, 1856, by Charlotte Birch-Pfeiffer, itself based on George Sand's novel *La petite Fadette*). Act I, Scene 2: Fanchon dances with her shadow.

(Mortised for Lettering.)

128. EAST LYNNE, by Clifton W. Tayleure (Brooklyn, 1862; N.Y., 1863; from Mrs. Henry Wood's novel). Scenes: Lady Isabel Carlyle is tempted to leave her home in company with Sir Francis Levinson (Act II, Scene 1); she dies repentant after returning as the governess Madame Vine (Act V, Scene 3). Also shown is her servant, Joyce, who has recognized her all along.

EAST LYNNE. 129. Act II, Scene 2: the Carlyles' garden; Lady Isabel on the point of eloping with Levinson. 130. Act IV, Scene 1: in the Carlyle home; "Madame Vine" hears Barbara, the new mistress of the house, sing the same song ("Then You'll Remember Me") she herself had sung when just married.

131. NOBODY'S DAUGHTER; OR, THE BALLAD SINGER OF WAPPING, by Chandos Fulton and Fred G. Maeder (N.Y., 1867; from Mary Elizabeth Braddon's novel *Diavola*). Act I, Scene 3: the ruins of Yarborough Tower. 132. INSHA-VOGUE; OR, THE WEARING OF THE GREEN (by William James Florence?; N.Y., 1867). Perhaps first performed by Florence and his wife.

133. SHAMUS O'BRIEN, THE BOULD BOY OF GLENGALL, by Thomas B. McDonough and Fred G. Maeder (N.Y., 1866). Written for and performed by the popular minstrel Dan Bryant.

134–135. OLIVER TWIST (one of many versions from Charles Dickens' novel). Bill Sikes murders his wife Nancy and accidentally hangs himself from a roof while attempting to elude justice.

136. THE CHILD STEALER, by Charles Gayler (N.Y., 1866; from a French play). Act III: the thieves' cellar; at the left is the former dealer in stolen children, who unwittingly sold her own daughter years ago; in the center, the sailor (who loves the grown-up daughter), fighting a duel with the villain, is treacherously plunged into a trap leading to the river. 137. OUT OF THE STREETS (by Charles Gayler, from his own novel; N.Y., 1868?). If adapted by Gayler, and from his novel, he adapted his own story very boldly, for the novel contains no scene like the illustration.

138. Clairvoyance; or, The Man with the Wax Figures (Brooklyn, 1867; from *L'homme aux figures de cire*, 1865, by Xavier de Montépin and Jules Dornay). Act V, Scene 4: the rearranged office of the public prosecutor; believing that the suddenly moving wax figures created by Vaubaron, the man he has persecuted, are really the ghosts of his dead victims, Rodille confesses all his crimes.

139. A DANGEROUS GAME, by A. W. Young (N.Y., 1867; from *Nos bons villageois*, 1866, by Victorien Sardou). Act I: by a stream in the village of Bouzy-le-Têtu; Henri Morisson, the amorous young man from Paris, has a run-in with the cantankerous villager Grinchu.

140. A DANGEROUS GAME. Act III: the home of the mayor; to protect the mayor's wife, Baroness Pauline, with whom he has had a rendezvous, Henri pretends to be a burglar who came to steal a necklace. 141. ENOCH ARDEN, by Julie de Marguerittes (N.Y., 1869; from Alfred Tennyson's poem). Enoch, on his desert island, looks out for a ship.

142. THE MENDICANT; OR, STRICKEN BLIND (N.Y., 1871; adapted from *La mendiante*, 1852, by Anicet-Bourgeois and Michel Masson). Act II: Jean-Paul Berghen, whose wife Marguerite has left him, consents to drive past her house and let her see their daughter, but a lightning flash blinds her. 143. SURF, by Olive Logan (Philadelphia, 1867; Boston, 1868; N.Y., 1870). Act III, Scene 2: social pleasures at the beach (Newport in the Boston version, Long Branch in the New York version). See Introduction, page x, for a description of this scene.

144–145. THE SCOUTS OF THE PRAIRIE (Buffalo Bill), by Ned Buntline (Edward Zane Carroll Judson) (Chicago, 1872; N.Y., 1873). The cast included Buffalo Bill himself, Ned Buntline himself, Texas Jack Omohundro and Madame Morlacchi, formerly head of the Morlacchi dance troupe.

146–147. DARLING; OR, WOMAN AND HER MASTER, by
Thomas B. De Walden (N.Y., 1872).

148–149. JACK HARKAWAY AFLOAT AND ASHORE (N.Y., 1873). One of a rash of Jack Harkaway plays, based on popular magazine stories. The Friday-like character was named Monday.

THROUGH FIRE, by Bartley Campbell (Philadelphia, 1872; N.Y., 1873). 150. Emblematic poster. 151. Act IV: California; the absconder Jarvis Josslyn, who has already shot one of the two men on his trail—former accomplice Gus Tivis—now tries to do away with the other—the man he framed, Bert Bristow.

THE TWO ORPHANS, by N. Hart Jackson (N.Y., 1874; adapted from *Les deux orphelines*, 1874, by Adolphe D'Ennery and Eugène Cormon). 152. Act I, Scene 1: outside the Normandy coach office near the Pont Neuf in Paris, 1784; the country girl Henriette is abducted by the minions of the lustful Marquis de Presles. 153. Act I, Scene 2: at the Marquis's Château du Bel-Air; the high-minded Chevalier Maurice de Vaudrey fights the Marquis to save Henriette.

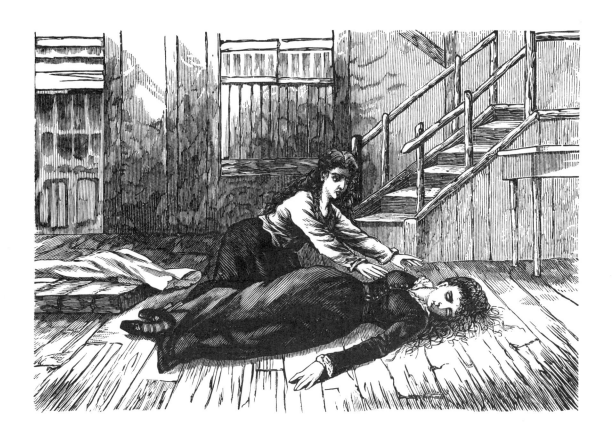

THE TWO ORPHANS. Two moments from Act III, Scene 2, interior of the dilapidated boathouse in which the hag La Frochard has secreted Henriette's blind sister Louise. 154. Louise locates Henriette, who had fainted when told her sister was dead. 155. The two dissimilar sons of La Frochard, the swaggering Jacques and the usually self-effacing Pierre, fight over Louise.

156. POLARIS (Boston, 1873). Possibly connected with Wilkie Collins' story "The Frozen Deep." 157. MARIA ANTONIETTA (Marie Antoinette), by Paolo Giacometti (N.Y., 1867, in Italian; Bologna, 1868). Act IV, Scene 6: a room in the tower of the Temple in Paris; on the eve of his execution, Louis XVI takes leave of his sister, wife and children.

158. LURLINE (an offshoot of *The Naiad Queen*, or the 1860 opera by William Vincent Wallace, or both?). 159. THE NAIAD QUEEN; OR, THE REVOLT OF THE NAIADS, by J. S. Dalrymple (London, by 1840; Philadelphia, 1840; N.Y., 1841). One of the scenes at the bottom of the Rhine.

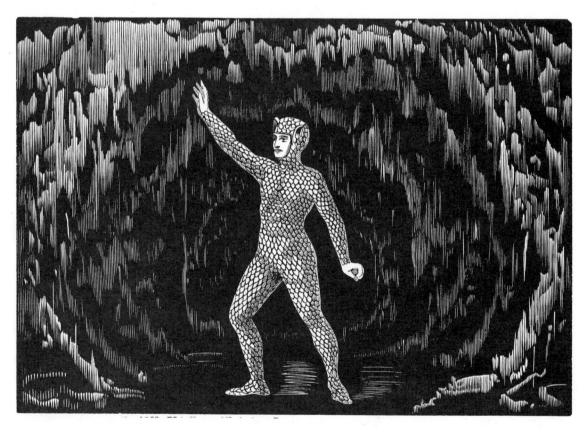

160–161. THE BLACK CROOK, by Charles M. Barras (N.Y., 1866). There were many elaborate ballet sequences, including some with undersea creatures.

162–163. THE BLACK CROOK. This extravaganza enjoyed a long initial run and several revivals at this time, and new acts and dances were constantly being introduced.

164. THE WHITE FAWN, by James Mortimer (N.Y., 1868). This probably shows Act I, Scene 3: the enchanted lake in the forest of sycamores. 165. LEO AND LOTOS (N.Y., 1873). Probably Act II: the grand bird ballet in the Kingdom of Birds.

166. Extravaganza scene; identified in the catalogue as from
one of the numerous stage versions of the Cinderella story.
167. Scene from an unspecified spectacle.

168. Scene from a spectacle with an Arabian Nights setting.

169. LA GRANDE-DUCHESSE DE GÉROLSTEIN, by Henri Meilhac and Ludovic Halévy; music by Jacques Offenbach (Paris and N.Y., 1867, in French). Act II: a room in the palace; the Grand Duchess and her courtiers exultantly plan revenge on the soldier Fritz, who has injured them all in various ways.

170. Les Brigands, by Henri Meilhac and Ludovic Halévy; music by Jacques Offenbach (Paris, 1869; N.Y., 1870, in French). Act I: mountainous terrain in Italy; the bandit chief Ernesto Falsacappa looks on as the young farmer Fragoletto pays suit to his daughter Fiorella.

JACK AND GILL WENT UP THE HILL, by George L. Fox (N.Y., 1866). 171. Simple Simon and the pieman. 172.

The title characters. 173. Scene 1: a frozen region; the Ice King rejoices in man's suffering during winter.

174. HUMPTY DUMPTY, by George L. Fox (N.Y., 1868). The characters in the center are the standard pantomime figures Clown, Pantaloon, Harlequin and Columbine; the bottom insert depicts Scene 8, a German billiard saloon.

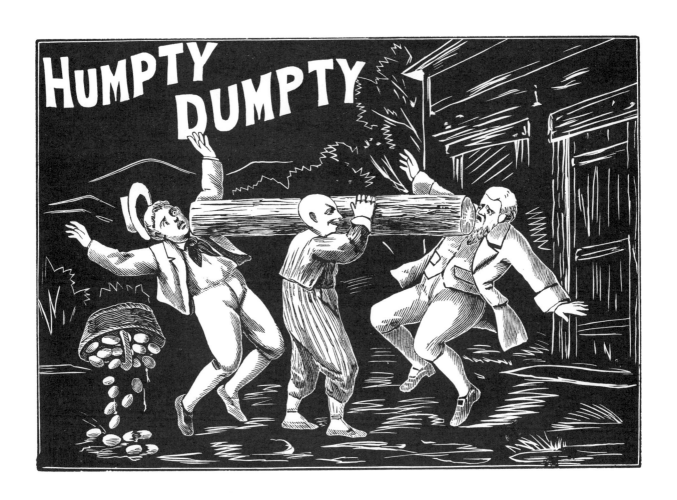

175–176. Humpty Dumpty.

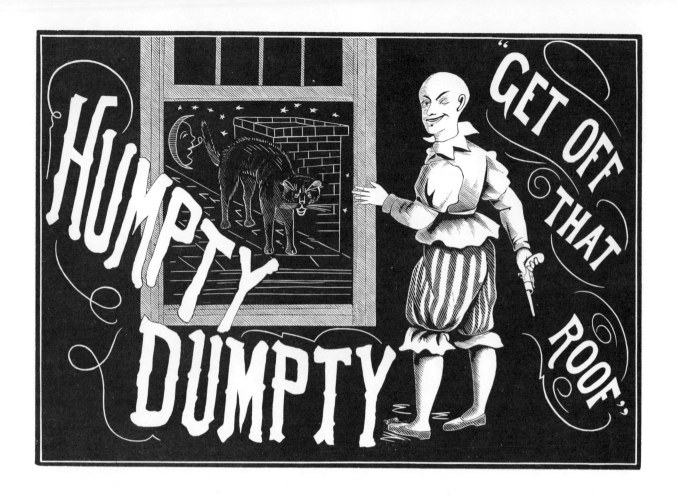

HUMPTY DUMPTY. 177. Possibly a scene leading up to the cat duet. 178. The cat duet.

179. HUMPTY DUMPTY. 180. THE THREE DWARFS (N.Y., 1874).

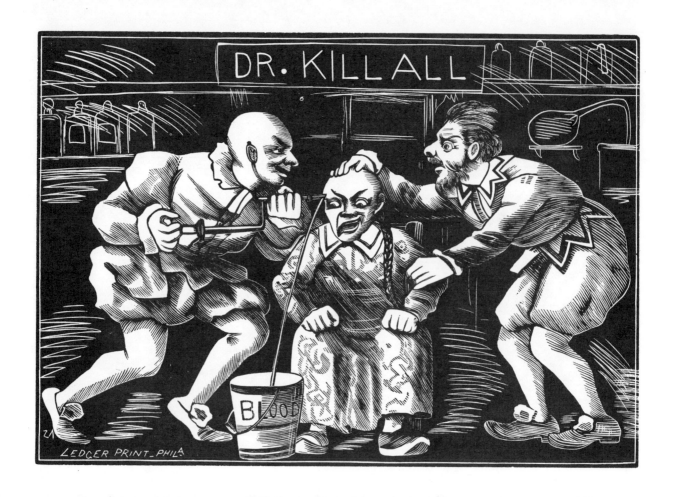

181–182. Typical pantomime scenes.

183. A typical pantomime scene. 184. Pantaloon.

185. Clown. 186. Columbine and Harlequin.

187. IXION; OR, THE MAN AT THE WHEEL, by Francis Cowley Burnand (London, 1863; Brooklyn, 1866; N.Y., 1868). The mortal Ixion visits the gods, among whom are Mars (in armor), Cupid (with bow and wings) and Minerva (with fan).

188. ALADDIN; OR, THE WONDERFUL SCAMP!, by Henry James Byron (London, 1861; N.Y., 1866). Aladdin bows down before the magician Abanazar, as the magic lamp hovers over them. 189. THE FIELD OF THE CLOTH OF GOLD, by William Brough (London, 1868; N.Y., 1869). Scene 5: the friendly tournament between Francis I of France and Henry VIII of England.

190. LUCRETIA BORGIA, M.D.; OR, LA GRANDE DOCTRESSE, by Henry James Byron (London, 1868; N.Y., 1868 or 1869). Scene 3: outside Lucretia's pharmacy in Ferrara; the Dook of Ferrara drinks with the medical student Gennaro. 191. PLUTO, by Henry Brougham Farnie (N.Y., 1869). The Lingards (William Horace Lingard and Alice Dunning) presented this burlesque in New York.

192. Much Ado About a Merchant of Venice, by John Brougham (N.Y., 1869). Act I: a street in Venice; Shylock discovers that his money and his daughter Jessica are both missing. 193. Sinbad the Sailor; or, The Ungenial Genii and the Cabin Boy, by Henry Brougham Farnie (N.Y., 1869). Probably shows Scene 3: the deck of the *Lively Polly*.

194. SINBAD THE SAILOR. Streamer. 195. THE FORTY THIEVES; OR, "STRIKING OIL" IN "FAMILY JARS," by Henry Brougham Farnie (N.Y., 1869). Based on the story of Ali Baba.

THE FORTY THIEVES. 196. Streamer. 197. Act II, Scene I:
the cave of the forty thieves.

198–199. Typical burlesque costumes.

200. THE BELLES OF THE KITCHEN, a variety sketch, written and performed by the Vokes family, about histrionically inclined servants (N.Y., 1872; earlier in England). 201. THE LITTLE FRAUD (also known as "A LITTLE FRAUD"), a variety sketch performed by Edward Harrigan with two successive partners, Sam Rickey and Tony Hart.

Two important dance groups who appeared both in variety
and in full-length musical pieces. 202. Josephine Morlacchi's
ballet company. 203. The Clodoche troupe.

204. The cancan, a dance craze of the late 1860s.

Two operas by Giacomo Meyerbeer to texts by Eugène
Scribe. 205. LE PROPHÈTE (Paris, 1849; N.Y., 1853). 206.
L'AFRICAINE (Paris, 1864; N.Y., 1865).

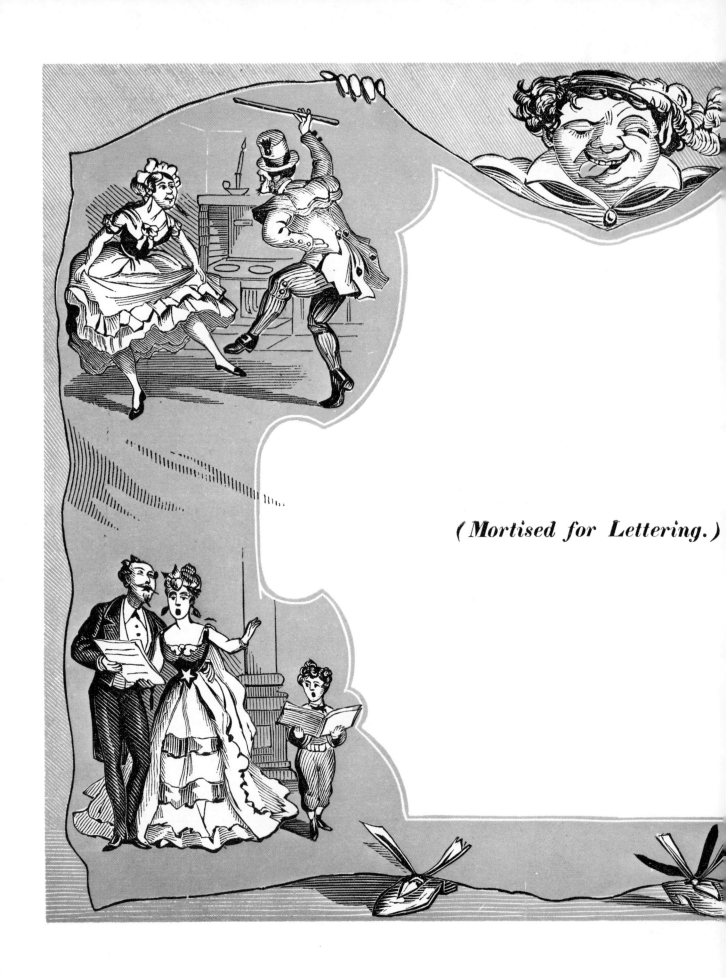

(Mortised for Lettering.)

207. Variety illustration, showing an Irish country dance, a singing family, a ballet troupe, and a minstrel clog dance.

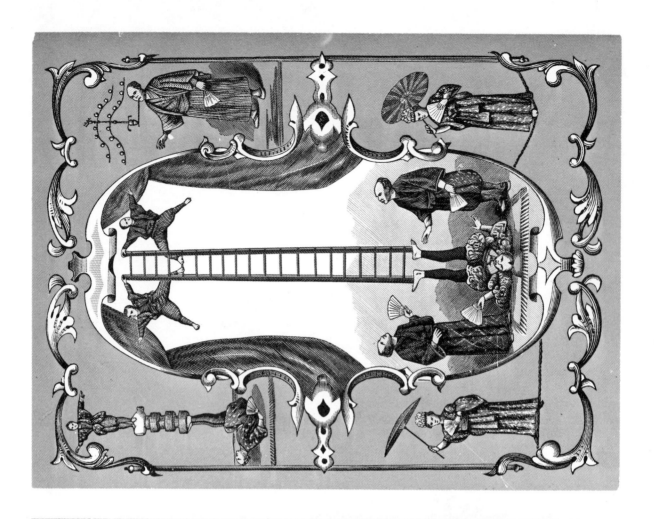

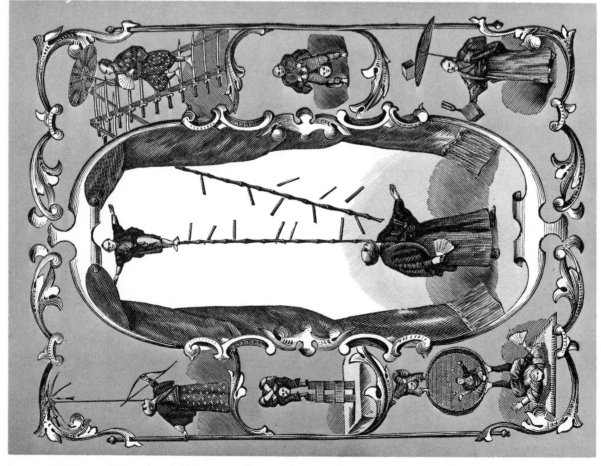

120   VARIETY ACTS AND THE CIRCUS

(Mortised for Lettering.)

210–211. Magicians.

(Mortised for Lettering.)

212. Trapeze artists in a theater.

213. The velocipede, a popular variety act of the period.
214. Punch and Judy hand puppets.

[Mortised for Lettering.]

215. Circus parade and acts.

216. Stage Irishman. 217. Irish girl.

218. Irish girl. 219. Dutchman (German).

STAGE TYPES   127

222. Eighteenth-century highwayman, such as Jack Sheppard. 223. Female Zouave.

224. Drummer girl. 225. Aladdin.

130   **STAGE TYPES**

M'ME CELESTE.

LUCILLE WESTERN.

228–229. Major actresses of the period.

ADELAIDE RISTORI.

230. The great Italian tragedienne Ristori. 231. William Horace Lingard, quick-change artist and singer who introduced several notable English music-hall songs to America.

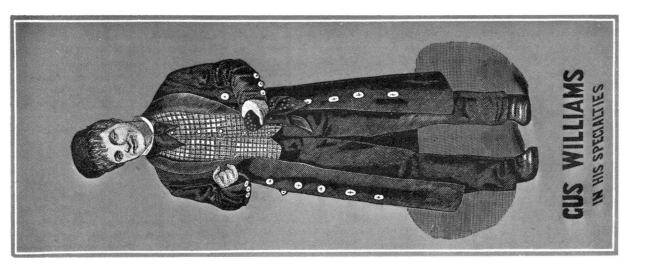

232. A famous "Dutch" comedian, Gus Williams. 233. One of the greatest names in the history of variety and vaudéville, Tony Pastor.

234–235. Variety performers.

236. This aerialist was actually a teenage boy whose family name was Farini. 237. Variety performers.

238–246. Assorted program cuts.

247–255. Assorted program cuts.

256–264. Assorted program cuts.

265–266. General illustrations.

267–268. General illustrations.

ADDITIONAL COMMENTS

The numbers are those of the illustrations.

1. The Philadelphia impresario Francis Courtney Wemyss commissioned the 1828 version while the novel was still in press. All the dramatizations of *The Red Rover* (at least seven in America and England) are garbled and take great liberties with the original.

3–4. This 1831 play was given new life in 1861 when an Albany, N.Y., production featured a female Mazeppa —Adah Isaacs Menken, who later played the role in many American cities and in London and Paris. Many actresses followed her lead.

5. The role of Matilde was wordless, having been written for the French dancer and actress Madame Céleste (Céline Céleste), whose English was still poor in 1831. Mute roles, performed as in a *ballet d'action*, were popular in the early nineteenth century—even in opera (*La muette de Portici*, by Auber, for instance)! The playwright Haines is also remembered for *My Poll and My Partner Joe*, 1835.

6. As frequently occurred, a subsidiary comic figure (the farmer) stole the show from the serious lawyer, and the farmer's role was built up over the years, the title eventually changing to *Solon Shingle*. The great portrayer of Solon in the period of the catalogue was John Edmond Owens.

7. In the play, the vision transparencies do not come into sight until after the *Freischütz*-like scene with the demon. Another subtitle that occurs is "The Witch of Castle More."

8. The illustration appears to combine two different act finales. The background action concludes Act II, but the foreground corresponds to the end of Act I, where settlers find the body of an Indian killed by Nick

and marked on the breast with his characteristic cross. The proper foreground figures for the ending of Act II would be renegades and unfriendly, but still living, Indians.

9. Miami was another of the great roles of Madame Céleste. "Green Bushes" is an old song by which characters in the play recognize one another.

10–12. Aiken's *Uncle Tom* was not the very earliest dramatic version, but the first important one and a model for those that established *Uncle Tom's* overwhelming popularity on the stage. Aiken's version was originally performed by the intermarried clan of the Howards and the Foxes, with little Cordelia Howard as Eva and George L. Fox, later the greatest American pantomime clown, as Phineas Fletcher. It has been claimed that this was the first play in New York to occupy an entire evening by itself.

13. During its long career, this play was known by several other titles.

14. The first New York Camille and Armand seem to have been Jean M. Davenport and F. B. Conway (brother-in-law of the famous actress Mrs. D. P. Bowers).

15–17. This was an entertainment in which Helen and Lucille Western, billed as the Star Sisters, each played many roles.

18–19. Note the difference in the appearance of the trees. Is 18, then, supposed to represent the killing of Louis by Château-Renaud? For one thing, that killing is not shown on stage; for another, in the script only five days intervene between the duels. Boucicault made this adaptation for Charles Kean (son of Edmund), manager of the Princess's Theatre. The play was also famous for its special "Corsican trap," which allowed the ghost to glide across the stage, and for its eerie "Ghost Melody" played by the theater orchestra.

20. This English adaptation, performed by Charles Kean, has also been attributed to Thomas William Robertson.

21–23. This later became known as *The Streets of New York*, and Boucicault also adapted it as *The Poor of Liverpool* and *The Streets of London*. The Five Points was a notorious slum on the Lower East Side. The action of the play reflects the actual financial panic of 1857.

24. In the original production, Agnes Robertson, Boucicault's wife, played Pauvrette, and Boucicault played the old soldier Bernard (seen at the right of the illustration).

25. Agnes Robertson played Zoe, and Boucicault played Wahnotee. Shirley Brooks's 1847 play *The Creole; or, Love's Fetters* has been named as a partial source, but the resemblance is not great.

26–27. Agnes Robertson played Eily, the "Colleen Bawn" (fair-haired girl), Boucicault was the horse-trading Myles-na-Coppaleen (Myles of the little horses), Laura Keene was Anne Chute. The water effect in this scene was created by translucent blue gauze.

28–29. This scene, for which Boucicault supplied the designs to the original set painter, involved intricate stagecraft: the interior of Shaun's cell swung around to reveal the exterior, then the outer wall moved downward as Shaun "climbed" it, until he "reached" the top. In the first London production, Agnes Robertson played Arrah, Boucicault played Shaun-the-Post (he delivered the mail), and John Brougham played Colonel Bagnal O'Grady. For this play Boucicault revived the old song "The Wearing of the Green," furnishing fiery new words. The nickname Arrah-na-Pogue signifies "Arrah of the Kiss."

30. The act identification and description of the illustration are based on a program and the original Scott novel. The play was also known as *The Trial of Effie Deans*. See Introduction, page xi. Agnes Robertson played Jeanie, Laura Keene was Effie, and Boucicault was the counsel for the defense.

31–33. Of the many stage versions of *Rip*, the most significant was the revision Boucicault prepared for Joseph Jefferson, who played it for some forty years.

34–35. Perhaps suggested by incidents in Mrs. Gaskell's novel *Mary Barton; A Tale of Manchester Life*.

36. Henry Irving played Scudamore in the original London production. Laura Keene played the title role in some American performances. Guilbert de Pixerécourt's 1802 play *La femme à deux maris* was probably the ancestor of this plot, but it is incorrect to call it (as has been done) a direct model for *Hunted Down*.

37. Possibly the first horse-racing play, this already featured drugging of the favorite horse, a last-minute substitute jockey and an actual view of the race, with cut-out horses in the background and a live horse brought on at the end.

38. This play also featured an escape from death under the wheels of a train—in London's then new "Underground." Augustin Daly, who had used the train scare in *Under the Gaslight* the year before, obtained a temporary injunction against *After Dark* when it came to New York, but the idea was not original with Daly.

39–40. The boat race in this play capitalized on the enormous publicity given to an actual Thames race in 1869 between Oxford and Harvard crews. The character of "Formosa," typical of the contemporary wealthy London courtesans of humble birth, was modeled on the real-life Mabel Grey. In London, Henry Irving played the villain. The subtitle "The Railroad to Ruin" plays on the title of the famous 1792 play by Thomas Holcroft, *The Road to Ruin*.

41–42. The original Katey in London was Rose Leclercq, who 26 years later created the role of Lady Bracknell in *The Importance of Being Earnest*.

44. "Rapparee" generally means bandit or renegade; here it is applied to patriotic Irish irregulars.

47–48. Written for the eminent actor John McCullough, this Civil War play was not unworthy of (or very different from) its vastly more popular counterparts of the 1890s that included Bronson Howard's *Shenandoah*, William Gillette's *Secret Service* and Clyde Fitch's *Barbara Frietchie*.

49. There were nineteenth-century rumors that Taylor had here appropriated a play by the Yankee comedian Josh Silsbee, who visited England at the time of the 1851 Exhibition. In Laura Keene's original production, she played Florence Trenchard. Dundreary was played by Edward Askew Sothern, who built this tiny role into a career (the illustration resembles him). The original Asa was Joseph Jefferson.

50. This lively play, full of low-life local color, is the source of Hawkshaw as a name for a detective. The original Bob Brierly in London was Henry Neville; in New York, William James Florence.

51. Henry Neville starred in this original production.

52. Kate Bateman starred in New York.

54. This play is also referred to as merely *Clancarty*.

55. Mrs. Bancroft (the former Marie Wilton) created the role of Mary Netley; John Hare, that of Petrovski.

56. Mrs. Bancroft was the first Polly Eccles. Robertson's successes were generally introduced to New York by Lester Wallack in his elegant theater, but William J. Florence beat him to *Caste*.

59–60. Mrs. (Madge) Kendal played the haughty Lady Clara in London. This was her only appearance in a London première of a work by her famous brother Tom Robertson. Harfthal, father and son, was a dual role.

61–62. Mrs. Bancroft was Naomi; John Hare, Beau Farintosh.

63–64. E. A. Sothern was the star in London.

67. Collins' novel was published in 1860, and dramatizations by others appeared within that year in London and New York. The description in the caption is based on the original novel, which does not contain a scene precisely like the illustration.

68. The act identification and description are based on the 1882 dramatization by A. Newton Field.

69–71. In Liverpool and London, Henry Irving played Redburn.

74. It was in the role of Tom Gilroy that the popular young English actor and clotheshorse Harry Montague, the first real "matinee idol," was introduced to American audiences. Boucicault had "discovered" him in England, and he was in the original cast of a few plays included here.

75–76. Later in the 1870s, E. A. Sothern, again building up a minor comic character (played by the author, Byron, in the first production), put on this play with the title *The Crushed Tragedian*.

77–79. The original London Job Armroyd was Henry Neville, with Adelaide Neilson as Nelly and the great comedian John Lawrence Toole as the servant Benjamin Blinker. Illustration 79 does not correspond exactly with the script.

80–81. Henry Irving was the original Robert Arnold, and Toole was in this London cast also. There is no pitched battle in the script such as the one in the illustration.

84. Description based on program.

87–88. The star was the outstanding tragedienne Adelaide Neilson. The play departs from the Scott novel.

93. There were numerous dramatizations of this novel. Possibly the one by Hazlewood did not come to America. The version seen by New Yorkers in 1863, by John Brougham, was called *The Mystery of Audley Court* and starred Mrs. D. P. Bowers, who played Lady Audley throughout the country for many years.

95–96. The Peep o' Day Boys were bands of United Irishmen involved in the agitation against England in the 1790s.

99. The catalogue identification is merely "Oonah," and I have found no script, but it is tempting to believe that this represents Falconer's *Oonagh*, which is credited with an original English run of less than one performance, the bored stagehands closing it down even before the audience could condemn it. If the play in the catalogue is the same, it enjoyed somewhat more glory in the United States. The literature on the subject mentions two possible sources for Falconer's play, an unspecified story by Maria Edgeworth and the novel *Fardorougha the Miser* (by William Carleton). The latter has a girl named Oona, or Una (who lives in Lisnamona and has a sweetheart), and two trials, but no scene like that in the illustration.

100. This was written as a vehicle for Lotta (Charlotte Crabtree), the sprightly young actress who first won fame in the mining camps of the Far West.

102. Brother Sam was a character frequently mentioned by Dundreary in *Our American Cousin* (as Sothern rewrote the role), and finally achieved a play of his own.

103–104. This play was the winner of a competition in 1866 (for the T. P. Cooke Prize of £100; Cooke had been a popular portrayer of nautical characters). The title of the play is parodied in the title of W. S. Gilbert's 1867 burlesque (of Donizetti's *La fille du régiment*) called *La Vivandière; or, True to the Corps*.

105–106. There were various nineteenth-century plays about Herne (who is mentioned prominently in Shakespeare's *Merry Wives of Windsor*, Act IV, Scene 4, and elsewhere), including an 1856 work by the American N. B. Clarke; I have associated these illustrations with Marchant's play only because of its date (close to the period of the catalogue) and his popularity (at least in England). I have seen no script, and the novel offers no scenes precisely like the illustrations. The conflicting legends about this haunter of Windsor Forest all seem to be Christian disguises of what was actually a pagan deity whose activities resembled the Teutonic "wild hunt" (can Herne be connected with the antlered god Cernunnos of the Celts?).

107. Brougham played Terry.

108–109. Description based on the novel.

110. Daly made this adaptation for the former child actress Kate Bateman, whose father H. L. (for Hezekiah Linthicum) Bateman brought Offenbach's operettas to New York and later brought Henry Irving to the Lyceum in London. Fanny Janauschek played the original, *Deborah*, in German in New York in the 1860s.

120–121. The adaptation has been credited to other hands than Daly's, including N. Hart Jackson's. The act identifications, descriptions and characters' names in the captions are based on the original French text by Sardou.

122–123. Said to have been the first American play on the subject of divorce.

124–125. The role of Cora was one of Clara Morris' first important opportunities to display the heavy emoting that became her specialty. Article 47 of the French penal code concerned strict police supervision of ex-convicts and limitation of areas in which they could travel and reside. The caption descriptions are partially based on a translation by Henry Llwellyn Williams, which may have been the origin of the (apparently different) adaptation attributed to Daly.

127. Waldauer was a St. Louis musician who made this adaptation (in New Orleans, 1860?) for the popular actress Maggie Mitchell, in whose repertoire it remained for decades.

128–130. The most enduring of all domestic melodramas, this naturally appeared in numerous versions, with the possibility of variations in acts and scenes. The Lady Isabel of the 1862 Brooklyn production (apparently the first on record in America or England) was Lucille Western, long associated with the role.

131. Scene description from a program.

133. Bryant also essayed Irish roles in straight plays during the 1860s.

134–135. *Oliver Twist* has been placed here (although British dramatizations begin in 1838) because of the huge success of a version played by Lucille Western and E. L. Davenport about 1866. This production has

repeatedly been called the first "combination": a large group or whole company of actors traveling independently with a play (not as a second, third, etc., company). Earlier, it was the rule for only a single star or a man and wife to travel and act with the local stock companies. The combination system was a major factor in the American theater for the remainder of the century.

136. This play was in Lucille Western's repertoire. The act identification and the description are based on a British adaptation, by W. E. Suter, in which the sorrowing mother is named Jane Rutherford; the sailor, Sydney Weston; and the villain, Joe Simpson.

138. Act identification and description from the original French text by Montépin and Dornay. The 1867 Brooklyn production starred the important tragedian Edwin Adams.

139–140. Act identification, proper names and descriptions from the original French text by Sardou. Augustin Daly made his own adaptation of this play in 1867, called *Hazardous Ground.*

141. In the 1872 dramatization of the poem made by Arthur Matthison (actually the basis of the catalogue illustration?), the scene depicted is the opening of Act IV. Edwin Adams starred in the 1869 version. Some version had been performed in Brooklyn in 1864.

142. Act identification and description from the original French text by Anicet-Bourgeois and Masson. Lucille Western was the 1871 star.

151. Description from a plot summary.

152–155. D. W. Griffith's 1922 film, *Orphans of the Storm*, was based on this play.

157. Giacometti also wrote *La morte civile*, in which Tommaso Salvini starred.

158–159. Lurline is the proper name of the Queen of the Naiads in Dalrymple's play. In the 1840 Philadelphia production, Charlotte Cushman led a marching group of fifty female warriors.

164–165. *The White Fawn* and *Leo and Lotos* were produced at the same theater (Niblo's Garden) as *The Black Crook*, but were not nearly so successful. The balletmistress and prima ballerina in *Leo and Lotos* was Katti Lanner (daughter of the Viennese waltz composer Josef Lanner), later an outstanding choreographer in London.

174–179. The ballerinas Rita Sangalli and Betty Rigl, who had appeared in the first production of *The Black Crook*, were in *Humpty Dumpty* when it opened.

187. In Lydia Thompson's New York production of 1868, she played Ixion, Pauline Markham was Venus, and Harry Beckett was Minerva.

188. It was the Worrell sisters (Sophie, Jennie and Irene) who presented this burlesque in New York in 1866. In the original London production, Aladdin was played by the burlesque star Marie Wilton, soon to become the highly respectable Mrs. Bancroft.

189. Presented in New York early in 1869 both by the Worrell sisters and by Mr. and Mrs. William J. Florence. In the original London production, Lydia Thompson played Earl Darnley, shortly before her first visit to America. The Field of the Cloth of Gold was a diplomatic meeting, in Flanders, 1520, between the monarchs of England and France.

190. This illustration shows the sign that the jolly medical students have hung outside the pharmacy: "Walker" (an English slang word connoting a bluff).

192. Brougham played Shylock.

193–197. Done by Lydia Thompson's company in New York. The expression "Family Jars" in the subtitle of *The Forty Thieves* no doubt refers to the 1822 play of that name by Joseph Lunn.

203. The Clodoche troupe were in *The Forty Thieves* in New York.

208–209. Japanese jugglers were first imported from their homeland by the impresario Richard Risley in 1866, by special arrangement with the Japanese government.

228. Lucille Western has been mentioned several times in these comments.

229. Madame Céleste was the original star of *The French Spy* and *The Green Bushes*.

230. Ristori was the star of *Maria Antonietta*.

232. Gus Williams was still active in the first decade of the twentieth century.

234. Davies appeared in *Leo and Lotos*.

ILLUSTRATIONS
BY PRINTER'S CATEGORIES

The numbers are those of the illustrations. The prices are those charged by the Ledger Job Printing firm in 1875.

POSTERS

One-Sheet
Black and White ($5.00 per hundred): 1, 7, 14, 18–19, 21, 26, 30, 34–35, 37, 55, 77–78, 80, 82, 90–94, 101, 103–104, 110–111, 113–114, 118, 126, 129, 134–137, 139–141, 149, 157, 161–163, 175–179, 181–183

Green or Blue ($7.00 per hundred): 159

Two Colors ($10.00 per hundred): 8, 22–23, 27, 36, 39, 42–44, 46, 48, 52, 57–60, 62–63, 67–68, 70, 72–73, 83, 88–89, 100, 102, 105–106, 109, 115, 117, 121–122, 127, 131, 142–143, 145–148, 151–156, 184–186, 195, 210–211, 219–221

Three Colors ($13.00 per hundred): 13, 28, 166, 180, 205–206

Four Colors ($17.00 per hundred): 2–3, 20, 31, 45, 53, 65–66, 71, 74–76, 99, 112, 120, 124, 130, 132, 158, 189–191, 197–200, 217, 222–227, 233

Five Colors ($18.00 per hundred): 203

Two-Sheet
Black and White ($10.00 per hundred): 10–11, 81

Two Colors ($20.00 per hundred): 6, 32, 40–41, 47, 85–86, 108, 150,* 170, 192, 201, 208–209, 214, 218, 231–235, 237

Four Colors ($34.00 per hundred): 4–5, 33, 87, 97–98, 119, 160, 167, 202

Three-Sheet
Two Colors ($30.00 per hundred): 125

Four Colors ($50.00 per hundred): 123, 193, 236

Four-Sheet
Two Colors ($40.00 per hundred): 215

Four Colors ($65.00 per hundred): 165

DODGERS (small handbills in two colors at $4.50 per thousand): 25, 107, 116, 128, 174

STREAMERS (long narrow horizontal bills)

Three-Sheet
Black and White ($15.00 per hundred): 144

Four-Sheet
Blue ($28.00 per hundred): 194

Six-Sheet
Blue ($42.00 per hundred): 196

PROGRAM AND CARD CUTS: 9, 12, 15–17, 24, 29, 38, 49–51, 54, 56, 61, 64, 69, 79, 84, 95–96, 133, 138, 164, 168–169, 171–173, 187–188, 204, 207,** 212–213, 216, 228–230, 238–268

Electrotypes of many of the poster cuts were available in the catalogue size at prices that varied with the number of colors and the size of the cut in the catalogue. Program and card cuts were available only in the form of electrotypes.

The "sheet" is the traditional size unit of posters. According to a 1916 British source (*Billposting*, ed. by Cyril Sheldon, Sheldon's Limited, Leeds), three standard measurements of the single sheet, all long in use among printers, were: 20 × 30 inches (double crown), 22½ × 35 (double demy) and 25 × 40 (double royal), the first being the most common. Two-sheet posters of these three varieties measured 30 × 40, 35½ × 45 and 40 × 50; three-sheets, 60 × 30, 67½ × 35½, 75 × 40.

* Only $10.00 per hundred.

** $8.00 per hundred.

ALPHABETICAL
LIST OF PLAYWRIGHTS

The numbers are those of the illustrations.

Aiken, George L., 10–12
Anicet-Bourgeois, 142
Augier, Emile, 63–64
Barras, Charles M., 160–163
Barrière, Théodore, 90
Belot, Adolphe, 124–125
Birch-Pfeiffer, Charlotte, 53, 127
Boucicault, Dion, 18–48
Brisebarre, Edouard, 21–23, 50
Brough, William, 189
Brougham, John, 107–109, 192
Buckstone, John Baldwin, 2, 9, 102
Buntline, Ned, 144–145
Burnand, Francis Cowley, 187
Byron, Henry James, 41–42, 69–76,
    188, 190
Campbell, Bartley, 150–151
Carré, Michel, 20
Chapman, Samuel H., 1
Collins, William Wilkie, 67–68
Cormon, Eugène, 152–155
Dalrymple, J. S., 159
Daly, Augustin, 110–125
de Marguerittes, Julie, 141
D'Ennery, Adolphe, 13, 24, 38, 152–
    155
Desnoyer, Charles, 24

De Walden, Thomas B., 146–147
Dornay, Jules, 138
Dugué, Ferdinand, 13
Dumas, Alexandre, *fils*, 14
Edwards, Pierrepont, 126
English, W. B., 15–17
Falconer, Edmund, 95–100
Farnie, Henry Brougham, 191, 193–
    197
Feuillet, Octave, 126
Florence, William J., 132
Fournier, Narcisse, 43
Fox, George L., 171–179
Fulton, Chandos, 131
Gayler, Charles, 136–137
Giacometti, Paolo, 157
Gilbert, William Schwenk, 65–66
Grangé, Eugène, 18–19, 38
Haines, John Thomas, 5
Halévy, Ludovic, 119, 169–170
Halliday, Andrew, 84–89
Hazlewood, Colin Henry, 90–94
Jackson, N. Hart, 152–155
Jones, Joseph Stevens, 6–7
Kock, Henry de, 90
Logan, Olive, 143
Maeder, Fred G., 131, 133

Marchant, Frederick, 105–106
Marston, John Westland, 101
Masson, Michel, 142
McDonough, Thomas B., 133
Medina, Louisa H., 8
Meilhac, Henri, 119, 169–170
Meyer, Henri-Horace, 43
Milner, Henry M., 3–4
Montépin, Xavier de, 18–19, 138
Mortimer, James, 164
Mosenthal, Salomon, 110
Nus, Eugène, 21–23, 50
Oxenford, John, 102
Phillips, Watts, 77–83
Reade, Charles, 43
Robertson, Thomas William, 55–64
Sardou, Victorien, 57–58, 116–118,
    120–121, 139–140
Scribe, Eugène, 205–206
Slous, Angiolo Robson, 103–104
Sothern, Edward Askew, 102
Tayleure, Clifton W., 128–130
Taylor, Tom, 49–54
Waldauer, August, 127
Wallack, Lester, 126
Young, A. W., 139–140

ALPHABETICAL
LIST OF PLAYS

The numbers are those of the illustrations. Only the main part of the title is given.

Africaine, L', 206
After Dark, 38
Aladdin, 188
Amy Robsart, 87–88
Arrah-na-Pogue, 28–29
Article 47, (L'), 124–125
Aventurière, L', 63–64
Belle Lamar, 47–48
Belles of the Kitchen, The, 200
Bergère des Alpes, La, 24
Black Crook, The, 160–163
Blow for Blow, 72
Bohémiens de Paris, Les, 38
Brigands, Les, 170
Brother Sam, 102
Camille, 14
Captain Kyd, 7
Caste, 56
Child Stealer, The, 136
Clairvoyance, 138
Colleen Bawn, The, 26–27
Corsican Brothers, The, 18–19
Cyril's Success, 73
Dame aux camélias, La, 14
Dangerous Game, A, 139–140
Darling, 146–147
Deborah, 110
Deux orphelines, Les, 152–155
Divorce, 122–123
Dreams, 59–60
East Lynne, 128–130
Elfie, 45–46
Elizabeth Prinzessin von England, 53
Enoch Arden, 141
Fanchon, the Cricket, 127
Faust and (et) Marguerite, 20
Fernande, 120–121
Field of the Cloth of Gold, The, 189
Firefly, The, 100
Flash of Lightning, A, 116–118

Flying Scud, 37
Formosa, 39–40
Forty Thieves, The, 195–197
Foul Play, 43
French Spy, The, 5
Frères corses, Les, 18–19
Frou-Frou, 119
Ganaches, Les, 57–58
Grande-Duchesse de Gérolstein, La, 169
Great City, The, 84
Green Bushes, The, 9
Griffith Gaunt, 111–113
Grille, Die, 127
Henry Dunbar, 51
Herne the Hunter, 105–106
Home, 63–64
Homme aux figures de cire, L', 138
House on the Bridge of Notre Dame, The, 90
Humpty Dumpty, 174–179
Hunted Down, 36
Ice Witch, The, 2
Innisfallen, 97–98
Inshavogue, 132
Ixion, 187
Jack and Gill Went Up the Hill, 171–173
Jack Harkaway Afloat and Ashore, 148–149
Jeanie Deans, 30
Lady Audley's Secret, 93
Lady Clancarty, 54
Lancashire Lass, The, 69–71
Leah, the Forsaken, 110
Leo and Lotos, 165
Léonard, 50
Little Em'ly, 85–86
Little Fraud, The, 201
Long Strike, The, 34–35

Lost at Sea, 41–42
Lost in London, 77–79
Lottery of Life, The, 107
Lucretia Borgia, M.D., 190
Lurline, 158
Maison du pont de Notre-Dame, La, 90
Maria Antonietta, 157
Marriage Certificate, The, 94
Mary Warner, 52
Mazeppa, 3–4
Mendicant, The (La mendiante), 142
Much Ado About a Merchant of Venice, 192
Naiad Queen, The, 159
New Magdalen, The, 68
Nick of the Woods, 8
Nobody's Child, 82
Nobody's Daughter, 131
Nos bons villageois, 139–140
Not Guilty, 80–81
Notre Dame, 89
Octoroon, The, 25
Oliver Twist, 134–135
On the Jury, 83
Oonagh, 99
Our American Cousin, 49
Ours, 55
Out of the Streets, 137
Partners for Life, 74
Pauvres de Paris, Les, 21–23
Pauvrette, 24
Peep o' Day, 95–96
People's Lawyer, The, 6
Perle noire, La, 116–118
Pluto, 191
Polaris, 156
Poor of New York, The, 21–23
Portefeuille rouge, Le, 43
Prière des naufragés, La, 13

Progress, 57–58
Prompter's Box, The, 75–76
Prophète, Le, 205
Pure Gold, 101
Pygmalion and Galatea, 65
Rapparee, The, 44
Red Light, The, 108–109
Red Rover, The, 1
Retour de Melun, Le, 50
Rip Van Winkle, 31–33
Romance of a Poor Young Man, The,

126
Roman d'un jeune homme pauvre,
  Le, 126
School, 61–62
Scouts of the Prairie, The, 144–145
Sea of Ice, The, 13
Shamus O'Brien, 133
Sinbad the Sailor, 193–194
Surf, 143
Three Dwarfs, The, 180
Three Fast Men, The, 15–17

Through Fire, 150–151
Ticket-of-Leave Man, The, 50
True to the Core, 103–104
'Twixt Axe and Crown, 53
Two Orphans, The, 152–155
Uncle Tom's Cabin, 10–12
Under the Gaslight, 114–115
Waiting for the Verdict, 91–92
White Fawn, The, 164
Wicked World, The, 66
Woman in White, The, 67